The Love Letters of

PERCY FRENCH

and more besides . . .

Watercolour by Percy French, The Twelve Pins, Connemara.

For Maddy, Sheridan and Pam, Mike and Karen,
Tristan, Ryan and Harrison.

The Love Letters of

Percy French

and more besides . . .

compiled by Alan Tongue

with a Foreword by Paul Muldoon

THE LILLIPUT PRESS
DUBLIN

First published in 2015 by The Lilliput Press, Ltd, Dublin

ISBN 9781-84351-6606

Set in Mrs Eaves Roman (text 10/12pt, captions 9/9pt) and Mrs Eaves Italic (letters 12/14pt)

Front jacket:	Envelope postmarked 10 June 1892, Stratford-on-Avon.
Front flap:	Photograph of French by William R. Kennan, 41 Grafton Street, Dublin.
Back jacket:	Still Life by Percy French (watercolour, 18 x 18cm).
Endpapers:	Montage of some of the original letters.
	'Lennie', by Walter Osborne, at the sketching class in June 1894.

Printed in Spain by GraphyCems

Design: Arnie Gormley Graphics, Belfast

Contents

Foreword

by Paul Muldoon

Percy French was one of the great Irish poets of the late nineteenth and early twentieth centuries, a writer who offers an insight into Irish society no less telling than Yeats or Kavanagh or MacNeice.

I first read him at Christmas, 1965, when a smarty-pants teacher at Saint Patrick's College, Armagh, awarded me a copy of *Prose, Poems and Parodies* by Percy French as a prize in, of all things, French. The humor would not have been lost on the poet, I'm certain, since he clearly had an insatiable appetite for fun and games. In his brilliant introduction to *Prose, Poems and Parodies*, Alfred Perceval Graves recounts that, despite the fact some men in Ireland 'are called "boys" to the end of their days,' Percy French was truly a boy at heart throughout his life. That he 'never went out without [his] bow and arrows' was a fact that endeared him to me immediately, since I myself was inseparable from a bow.

Even if French had written nothing but parodies, as in Longfellow's great bowman *Hiawatha* (itself a parody of sorts of the Finnish national epic), his place in literary history would be secure:

> And the lovely Minnehaha
> Put her arms around her lover,
> Said, 'You are a top hole angel;
> But unless we get a motor,
> How am I to show my sables?'
> 'Motors cost a lot of money,'
> Said the cautious Hiawatha;
> 'Even when you do the driving,
> There's the upkeep and the petrol.'

By the time we include 'The Mountains of Mourne', 'Phil the Fluther's Ball', 'Eileen Oge', 'Gortnamona', 'Slathery's Mounted Fut', 'Are Ye Right There, Michael?' and 'Come Back, Paddy Reilly' we have a major literary achievement.

The character who presents himself in the letters to Miss Sheldon is very much of a piece with the wry, slightly rueful, protagonist we recognize from so many of the songs. There's the character who reports that 'I went to Venice yesterday & found it rather disappointing,' reminding us that French was, after all, a former Inspector of Drains. There's the character who announces 'Mullingar took to me kindly last night & I am giving a show tonight at the Mullingar lunatic asylum. They say I will be quite 'en rapport' with my audience.' There's the character who signs off as 'ever your insatiable old footerer'.

Percy French's self-deprecatory instinct to describe himself as a 'footerer' is not one in which we need support him. His work reminds us forcibly that *The Birds* of Aristophanes is no less serious than *The Bacchae* of Euripides merely because we've had a good laugh along the way.

Preface

Whilst attending the funeral in 1993 of Ettie French, the eldest daughter of William Percy French and his wife Lennie, I was privately handed an envelope containing handwritten letters, and was told that Ettie had left these to me. They turned out to be the letters that her father had written to her mother whilst he was courting her over a period of a year and a half from May 1892. We have to thank Lennie and Ettie for keeping these letters safe.

I passed the letters on to the Percy French Society to add to their memorabilia, by then housed in the Castle Museum, Bangor, North Down. There the letters remained until recently I decided to present them to the public.

I am grateful to Courtney Kenny, great-nephew of Percy French, for giving his approval to the project, and to the trustees of the Percy French Society for releasing this memorabilia. I am also very grateful to Jonathan and Jessica Hickman of Burmington House for their help in tracing the original viewpoints of the watercolours. I also thank Leanne Briggs, the curator of the memorabilia, for helping to collate all the various documents referred to in the letters. Thanks are due also to my publisher Antony Farrell for taking on this book and especially for his suggestion that I should track down the designer who worked on my previous book, Arnie Gormley. I am so grateful to Paul Muldoon for his fitting contribution.

Gentle, and very much of their time, these letters, which are being published for the first time, show French attempting to build on his career prospects simultaneously in Dublin and London, travelling between boarding houses in Baldoyle and Chelsea. The letters also clearly show that, far from being the 'West Briton' that some erroneously later dubbed him in the new Republic, he was a supporter of Home Rule. Having been attracted to landscape painting since his Cavan days, when the eruption of Krakatoa produced spectacular sunsets around the world for a few years, French is now studying artworks in galleries, painting landscapes and seascapes from life and in the studio, and sending his work for exhibition. We follow his visits to the theatre and agonise with him as he submits scripts to theatrical agents for musical comedies, plays and sketches. He is also an occasional contributor to *The Irish Cyclist*, a journal published in Dublin by his friend R.J. Mecredy. I hope these letters will throw new light on a remarkable man.

Alan Tongue, Largysillagh, 2015

Introduction

'Are ye right there, Michael?' How often has this headline appeared in the Irish press if someone called Michael is in the news or if national train delays occur. So much of Percy French's writing has crept into the Irish vernacular: 'Come Back, Paddy Reilly, to Ballyjamesduff, come home, Paddy Reilly, to me'; 'Where the Mountains of Mourne sweep down to the sea'; 'Oh, hadn't we the gaiety at Phil the Fluther's Ball!'

Who was this man? For me he was the most multi-talented Irishman: songwriter (words and music), entertainer, poet and painter. And by all accounts he was a truly lovely man, always ready to talk after his opening gambit, 'How's the old complaint?'

Born on 1 May 1854 at Cloonyquin in Co. Roscommon, his father a Justice of the Peace and High Sheriff and his mother the daughter of a Church of Ireland clergyman, as a child he was always entertaining the family with his fashioning of animals from bread and later with his comic writings and drawings. In *Chronicles of Percy French*, compiled by his sister Emily after his death in 1920, he writes about how his supposed genius at mathematics led him down the path to becoming a civil engineer.

His preferred choice of rambling entertainer and watercolour artist thus happened relatively late in life. His first paid employment, as Inspector of Loans to Tenants in Co. Cavan, referred to by him as 'Inspector of Drains', gave him time to write plays and act in them, compose comic songs and paint. It also gave him time to continue his love of tennis. This is where he met the young lady who was to become his first wife, Ethel Armitage Moore. They were married in 1890 during his time as editor of *The Jarvey*. A year later she died in childbirth, their baby dying a week later.[1] This sparked off a series of what he later, with his trademark play on words, called his pathetic poems.

French moved away for a time but eventully returned to Dublin, where his second musical comedy, *The Marriage of Eva and Strongbow*, was presented in May 1892. One of French's singers in Dublin was the mezzo-soprano Alyce Lindé, and while performing in *Strongbow* she invited a friend from her former boarding school in England to stay with her. The friend was Helen Sheldon, aged twenty-three and from Burmington, Warwickshire.[2] Ettie French, in her book entitled *Willie* about her famous father, writes that

> Soon Willie was visiting the house, ostensibly to give guitar lessons to Miss Lindé, but thoughtfully bringing an instrument for her friend as well. It was Lennie's cheerfulness, and especially her laugh, that first attracted him.[3]

Ettie tells us that

> Lennie had vowed in her youth never to marry a widower, or a man with a moustache, or one called William. When it came to the point she did all three without regret, but while they were engaged she must have tried to uphold her vows in one direction, for his letters to her for a short while are signed "Percy". But obviously Willie could not cope with the alien name, and he reverted to the old signature after a month or two.

Lennie was born on 31 July 1868 at Burmington, Warwickshire, the daughter of Jonathan Sheldon, miller, and his wife Mary Clementina Sheldon, *née* Tribe. Lennie's mother Mary died the following year, 1869, aged twenty-two, after the birth of her second child Ethel Grace. Jonathan remarried in July 1874, when Helen was six years old, and she was then brought up by her stepmother Rosabel.[4] Lennie meets French at age twenty-three. Her only other sibling, her younger sister Ethel,[5] is already married.

Lennie at six months, with her parents.

As our story starts, the following press interview with French gives a clear account of what he is up to . . .

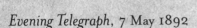

Evening Telegraph, 7 May 1892

AN "UP TO DATE" INTERVIEW

No. XXXI. - Mr. W. Percy French

"Strongbow" a Great Success.

Hints About His Next Move.

[SPECIAL TO THE "EVENING TELEGRAPH."]

It goes without saying that to write even a moderately succesful book of words for a comic opera is a task which requires both originality and wit. Just at present these productions are more or less the rage in Dublin, and it is reported that there are several in the stage of incubation. Dr. Collisson and Mr. French, however, were the first to take the field, but long before Mr. French's name was associated with "The Knight of the Road" he was widely known as a writer of humorous songs, and of clever lawn tennis skits, which were much appreciated by the patrons of the Fitzwilliam Square tournaments. Mr. French is a graduate of Trinity College, and by profession a civil engineer, but if there are few persons who can write as clever a song, he says himself that "there are many able to construct a better bridge..."

Your "Dublin up to Date" proved a very decided hit; how did the idea of giving the entertainment originate?

Mr. French - Attending one of Harry Furniss's lectures illustrated with caricatures, it struck me that with Mr. Orpen's assistance I could do something to amuse the Dublin people. We gave our entertainment at the Castle, and His Excellency was so much pleased with Mr. Orpen's lightning sketches in water colours that he expressed a wish to purchase it.

It was stated that you were going to do the provinces - has that scheme fallen through?

Mr. French — The production of "Strongbow" interfered with it, but in any case I have not as yet been able to arrange with regard to a business manager, and I regret to say I am very ignorant on business matters myself — almost as ignorant as I am of politics, but my want of knowledge on the last named subject I think rather an advantage than otherwise.

Which of your songs have you found the most successful?

Mr. French — "Slattery's Mounted Fut" was purchased by Messrs. Pigott. "Abdallah-Bulbul-Ameer" has had the largest circulation, but this brought small gain to me, as it was pirated by a London house, and I have twice seen it illustrated in London papers without any name being attached. The last war song in "Dublin up to Date" is going very well.

With regard to pirating of course you have legal redress?

Mr. French — Undoubtedly, but this involves expense and other difficulties, and as I before mentioned I am not a good business man.

The general experience of persons who live by the pen is that literature is not a very lucrative calling - perhaps you have been more fortunate?

Mr. French — Well, I have made writing pay, and am at last able to let other irons cool. It is now some years since I made out a long list of all my friends and sent them post-cards to say a work of mine was on sale at all the booksellers. They replied asking for a gratis copy, and saying they would tell their friends! What they told their friends I don't know; but none of them bought the booklet.

You edited The Jarvey I think for some time?

Mr. French — Yes, for two years which is about the usual duration of the life of an Irish comic paper. It started, however, with many things against it. The name was not a good one, and we had barriers of prejudice to break down, which, though we won many friends, we did not succeed in doing before our exchequer gave way. I greatly fear that London and New York have absorbed our best humourous talent, and am certain that a paper to pay now-a-days must be full of personalities — a sort of writing I take no interest in. Another reason that a Dublin comic paper seems doomed to fail is that it is impossible to get it properly published. Local shopkeepers much prefer inducing their customers to buy a London publication.

Before leaving Mr. French I had an opportunity of inspecting some water-colours which decorate the walls of his study, and are his own work. A piece of moorland scenery by him is exhibited at present in the Hibernian Academy.

First produced at the

QUEEN'S ROYAL THEATRE,

Under the Management of Mr. ELLIS JONES,
On Monday, May 2nd, 1892

STRONGBOW;

OR,

BRIDE OF THE BATTLEFIELD.

——:o:——

Dramatis Personæ:

DERMOD MACMORROUGH (King of Leinster) ... Mr. H. A. WEST.

HENRY II. ....(King of England).... Mr. GEORGE CRAWFORD.

ROBERT FITZSTEPHEN } Knights { Mr. FREDERICK FLINT.

RAYMOND Le GROS } { Mr. THOMAS.

CELLARIC..........(Cellarer to King Dermod)..Mr. J. KNOX FOOTE.

A HARPER.............................Mr. W. PERCY FRENCH.

A RETAINER.........................Mr. VEREKER EDWARDES.

STRONGBOW........(Earl of Pembroke)..Mr. HENRY BEAUMONT.

PHILIPINA } Ladies of the English Court {....Mrs. BETHAM.

VALERIE } {..Miss PRESCOTT.

AMAVE............. {........Miss ALYCE LINDE.

LURA................ } Bridesmaids {..Miss ISABEL MADDOCK.

AVEELE .... {..Miss EDITH GRANDISON.

CLEENAGH........(King Dermod's Cook)..........Miss MADDOCK.

RUELLA ....(the Harper's Daughter)........Miss GRANDISON.

DEVORGILLA (wife of Ruarc, King of Breffni) Mdme. JEANIE ROSSE.

AND

EVA ....(Daughter of King Dermod)......Miss DUBEDAT.

The Bishop, Acolytes, Kerns, Knights, Standard Bearers, Retainers,
Ladies of the English Court, Bridesmaids.

ACT I.—Banquetting Hall in Castle of King Dermod MacMurragh,
at Ferns, ...taine.

ACT II.—Court of King Henr

ACT III. Scene I.—The Camp

Scene II.—Interior of the Rin

Scene III.—The B

TIME, 11

The Scenery painted by Mr. Small,
executed by Mrs. Glenville, Dublin ; the
The whole produced under the direction

The cast list for *Strongbow* at the
Queen's Royal Theatre, pictured.
The libretto includes these lines:

Love now and for ever,
  Folding thee to my heart,
Ever to cheer thee, ever be near thee,
  Never on earth to part.

Dear Miss Sheldon,

　　I don't begin quite as warmly as I could wish but I am only waiting for leave.
My delight in your society is sufficiently obvious but I have no wish to force my attentions
where they are unwelcome. You would scarcely believe what a difference you made in my
life during the 2nd invasion of Strongbow.[7] The Doctor [8] – who is practising roulades at
my elbow on the most appalling type of lodging house spinet – used to wonder how it was
I was never dispirited at the sight of an empty house – I saw no vacant space, only your
bright smile everywhere.

　　This simile gives rather an exaggerated idea of the extent of your smile – I say this
to make you laugh. I used to love to hear you. Yours is the merriest & pleasantest laugh
I ever heard.

　　I can't write anything coherent or consecutive just now, but am just putting down
what comes into my head. Will you do the same when you write to me, we will get to know
each other sooner. The love I have for you is of a kind that does a man good, not the mere
desire that men feel for beauty, but the longing for your companionship, comradeship, the
longing for the right to work for you & make your life pleasant: so on missionary grounds
alone, let me live on in the sunshine.

　　A great city has many temptations & society's laws seem different for men &
women, for us there is no talisman like loving a pure & beautiful girl. You mustn't infer
from all this that without this amulet I would or have ever walked in evil ways. What
I mean is that the very thought of vice seem an insult to a man who really loves.

　　You asked me last night if I ever get angry – a man once made a suggestive joke
before my little wife – the most crystal souled girl that ever lived – that man walks a little
lame now & says I have a frightful temper!! aha! oho! Oh dear I wish I could see your
sunny face, you can't think how I enjoyed taking you to the Gaiety [9] & how delightful it
was to have you resting on my sofa – I like to think of it as mine. I wonder how much that
hand clasp meant when we parted at Stafford, pity for my forlorn state? Oh I know what
a paradise earth can be & what a wilderness it may become. People sometimes envy me my
life but they have little reason to do so – unless I have someone to work for I find life very

empty. I don't ask you to love me, I only tell you of my love for you & hope you may return it. Nor can I represent myself as a very eligible suitor, but I have already made a name for myself & that means capital in the literary world of today. When I saw you kneeling last Sunday in the cathedral I thought what a guiding star you would be to a pilotless bark of eccentric rig –

> *'Ever drifting drifting drifting*
> *on the shifting*
> *currents of a restless main.'*

Write and tell me how you got home & if you had any difficulty in getting your ticket for Worcester. The pleasure of having someone to look after & take a ticket for made me oblivious of such a minor detail as what station you were going to. 'Apropos des bottes' **10** *(observe my familiar use of foreign tongues) I have never seen Shakespeare's or Miss Sheldon's birthplace* – both places of great interest to your far too distant admirer*

W. Percy French

*are they on view next Sunday?

French at this time.[11]

70 Redesdale Street
Chelsea S.W.

Dear Miss Sheldon
Do please write to me
I was hoping for a line
this morning but nothing
came except letters from
agents (theatrical) who
seem anxious to make
my fortune.

I am only anxious about
one thing – can you ever
care for me? Do let me have
a conclusive reply – and yet
I can hardly hope – there
seems to me every reason
why I should love you &
no cause why you should care
for me. If I had been less

70 Redesdale Street
Chelsea S.W.
[May 1892]

Dear Miss Sheldon,

Do please write to me. I was hoping for a line this morning but nothing came except letters from agents (theatrical) who seem anxious to make my fortune.

I am only anxious about one thing – can you ever care for me? Do let me have a conclusive reply – and yet I can hardly hope – there seems to me every reason why I should love you and no cause why you should care for me. If I had been less in love with you I might have been a pleasanter companion, but you will make allowances, won't you.

I have started the musical play & am trying to work out the plot, but find it impossible to settle down to anything, until I know if there is anyone to work for besides myself.

You will see & hear a tourist next Sunday, in Shipston church, whose majestic proportions, classical features & rich apparel will recall the appearance of Erin's only librettist. The atmosphere of London is more repugnant to me than I expected. The Doctor and I went to the Gaiety last night to see the latest thing in burlesques, we agreed that the country air would be better for us. There is no performance I enjoy like 'Les Cloches de Corneville' [12] or the two nights you came to see Strongbow. [13] I find absence has the contrary effect on me to what you prognosticated.

The Doctor wants me to come with him to interview Col. Mapleson [14] about the production of 'Strongbow', so I must conclude this chatter to my regret – & oh! I hope to yours – a little – too.

I sent you an improving book on Tuesday which I trust arrived safely. Please don't think that anything I send you is from a desire to ingratiate myself – I do it because it gives me pleasure. I wish I could write a more amusing letter but all my fun has fled while this uncertainty prevails. It is only when I am near you that I can forget & be happy.

your devoted

W. Percy French

70 Redesdale Street in 2014.[15]

La Belle Souris.

Opéra Comique in Three Acts.

Composer. Señor Gustary. Librettist. Percy French.

Characters.

Duchess of Sol. Formerly a famous Danseuse, known as "La Belle Souris" a widow.

Consuelo. Daughter of General Lauriston, betrothed to Don J.de Castro.

Admiral Sir Patrick. O'Halloran K.C.B.

Count of Estrella. Nephew of Duchess, and cousin of Consuelo.

Principino de Capri. A Neapolitan Noble. ⎫ Old Admirers of

Commendatore. A Neapolitan Impresario. ⎬ "La Belle Souris"

Don Jaime de Castro. A Spanish financier, and Carlist agent. ⎭

General Lauriston. (A widower) father of Consuelo whose mother was a Spanish lady.

Guests- Students- Gypsies- Soldiers etc.

Act.1. Lauriston Castle. Scotland.

Act.11. The Same.

Act.111 Village near Granada. Spain.- Duchess's Chateau on left Inn on right. Church in background.

70 Redesdale Street
Chelsea S.W,
[31 May 1892]

Dearest Lennie,

After an uneventful journey – but no – a penny a liner never goes across the road without seeing something worth recording. Well, after the train had slowly dragged itself away from your enthralling smile your father [16] & I discussed the state of the country the crops & the political outlook till we got to Moreton.[17] Having arrived at that well known seat of learning, Mr Sheldon with a decisive grasp of the situation which reminded me of 'the man of destiny' suggested that I should telegraph my advent to the Authors' Society. This having been done we discoursed on the subject nearest my heart. Mr S addressed the meeting at some length on the manifold perfections of his daughter, drawing attention at the same time to the pecuniary embarrassment of his own position. Mr F rising amid a storm of dust remarked that he entirely agreed with the last speaker concerning the manifold charms of Miss Sheldon, she was a girl any man might be proud of (applause) and as to any prospect of fortune he was of opinion that money did not constitute happiness (hear hear) so if the lady cared to share his (Mr F's) worldly wealth he would feel that she was doing him an honour (loud & prolonged cheering). If the rest of this letter is rather incoherent I must tell you that an ex dragoon whom I knew in former days has just turned in to breakfast & is telling me tales of battle, murder & sudden death. I found on arriving at the Authors' Club that the dinner was on the 31st (tonight) so I can't give you an account of it yet. Dr C has also turned up in a very sleepy condition, having been to a dance last night. He wants to engage me for a concert tour & seems surprised to hear I am engaged to you. Expect me on Friday & do come to meet me. I used to like London but now there is no place like Burmington House. Write me a line whenever, like Mrs Gamp,[18] you 'feel so dispozed'. I haven't filled this letter with endearing terms, but we are both of us reserved & I think you must know by this time how you have brightened my life.

Goodbye my love
ever your insatiable
old footerer Percy

My kind regards to Mr & Mrs Sheldon.[19] You may tell them they have impressed me favourably – very favourably indeed.

Watercolour by Percy French from the driveway at Burmington House. The facade of the house is on the left, with the columns unfinished, work in progress.

Burmington House in 2014.[20]

My dearest Jennie

Your first love letter arrived this morning – it was short but sweet I am glad to hear you miss me, let me have more of your society when I return (oh dear! oh dear! I hear you say). Well the great dinner came off at the Holborn restaurant yesterday evening. I wore my black, cut rather low & filled in with 3 ply linen. I also wore a false smile to ingratiate myself with the company & help to conceal my ears. a harlequin set of

My dearest Lennie

    Your first love letter arrived this morning – it was short but sweet. I am glad to hear you miss me, let me have more of your society when I return (oh dear! oh dear! I hear you say). Well, the great dinner came off at the Holborn restaurant yesterday evening. I wore my black, cut rather low, & filled in with 3 ply linen. I also wore a false smile to ingratiate myself with the company & help to conceal my ears. A harlequin set of studs & hair parted on the bias completed my costume. The above is meant to be funny so please smile. I send you the menu & some lightning sketches of the celebrities. Mrs Thring I found rather uninteresting, but Sheridan Knowles I got on with very well, he had just published a novel & gave me a lot of information on the subject. Tell your mother the wines were all excellent. I know this from the clear state of my head this morning. The speeches were not very brilliant with the exception of Stockton's who told a Yankee story very well. Corney Grain **21** *gave a couple of songs in his best form but I was not asked to sing. No matter! – a day will come, ha! ha! when they will ask me to sing & then – let them beware!*

    There is not much more to tell you about the dinner – it was a good thing to do however, as it is encouraging to find that these great literary lions are very like ordinary mortals, French, Brindley, Whitton &c. Dr Collisson & I went to Venice **22** *yesterday & found it rather disappointing. The grand 'spectacle' is too long for a picture & Venice itself is too cramped for our enlarged views. I thought of sending you some rare Italian gems to sparkle in your raven tresses, but saw nothing worthy of such a position – neat way out of it, that. However I have got a light guitar & a lighter case for you, so I'm not so near – ah me, I wish I was, but near or far I am always – darling Lennie – your loving Percy*

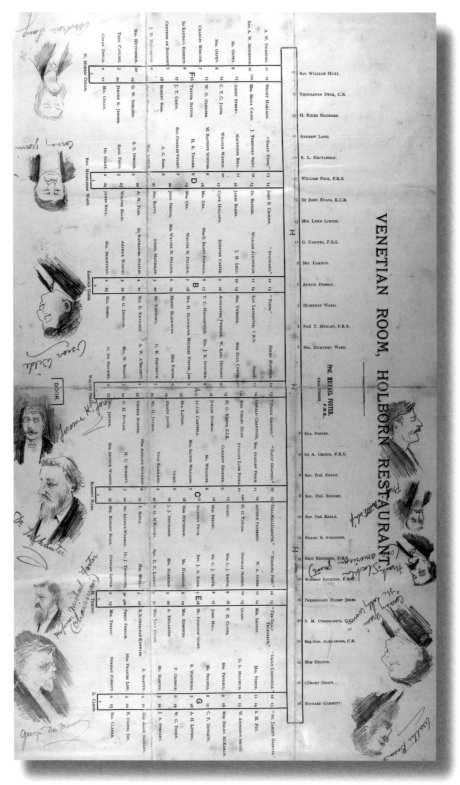

Previous page:

Seating layout for Incorporated Society of Authors' Annual Dinner, 31 May 1892.

Sketches by French, clockwise from right, of himself, Professor Nettleship, Frank Stockton, Corney Grain, Walter Besant, George du Maurier, Professor Michael Foster, Dr Todhunter, Jerome K. Jerome, Oscar Wilde, Corney Grain, Andrew Lang.

The signatures are all genuine.

Lennie at this time, by Walter Osborne.[23]

70 Redesdale Street
Chelsea S.W.
[June 1892]

Dearest Lennie

The proofs have just arrived & fail to recall the pretty Miss Sheldon that my mind's eye remembers. I think an action for libel might be brought against Graham – he can't be a descendant of Bonnie Dundee if this is all he can do. However I have marked the one I like best with a X so let me have one with all possible speed. The Great concert went off very well & I actually succeeded in making a row of old ladies smile. I gave them my sketch of a penny reading & afterwards 'Soldiers Three' **24** & the 'Starving Man', **25** the latter being encored. Collisson and I are to meet D'Oyly Carte **26** next week to give him an idea for Strongbow. If you could only march in with a banner & your hair down he would buy it on the spot. Mrs Smith, Alyce Lindé & Lord Bovril were at Negroni's concert & congratulated me on the 'pearl' I had captured' (do you 'capture' pearls?). Lord B. seems anxious to elope Miss L. before Henry III secures her. The Dr and I went to Lady Windermere's Fan last night, **27** a very clever piece, but gives rather a deplorable view of London society. The lecture the Duchess gives to Lady W. on 'those creatures men' & the talk in Lord Darlington's smoking room on 'Women' is racy enough for Aunt Flora. I left that giddy one at Paddington, having procured her a hansom & seen to her baggage. She got out at Oxford & I thought she had 'gone from my gaze like a beautiful dream about a pie' – but we were only shunting so she illumined my horizon once more laden with provisions. I sent you a guitar book yesterday which I hope will suit. This is a short & not very entertaining epistle but I am trying to get a lot of work done & run away from London. Kindest regards to Mr & Mrs Sheldon & much love to yourself

from your loving Percy

1.

We soldiers are a terror to the foe boys
And though I'm on the shelf
Such a warrior was I, when I let my rifle fly
I've often been a terror to myself
'Twas just before the battle
We heard the sergeant say
Be sure that you come, when you hear the drum—
We came—we came away

CHORUS.

For we don't like to hear the bullets rattle in the battle
And we don't like to hear the cannons roar— any more—
But we'll gather on the gory field of battle
When the cruel war is o'er

2.

There was me and Hector Mooney and O'Hara
Three soldiers bold and gay
And we swore with one accord we would never draw a sword
But we'd always draw our pay
When the order came for marching
And to get into fighting trim
Beneath our breath as we marched to death
We sang the soldiers hymn. (CHORUS)

3.

They told us we were bound for death or glory
So we kept a sharp look out
Says Mooney, "I declare the death is everywhere
But the glory never seems to be about"
We were not in the front boys
When the army charged along
But beneath a cock of hay on that memorial day
You might have heard this song. (CHORUS)

4.

Then me, and Hector Mooney, and O'Hara,
We all march home again
And we tell about the fight and the deeds of might
We did in our last campaign
You see this long red scar lads
I've got behind my ear
It was not a sabre's edge, it was dashing thro' a hedge
With the foemen in the rear. (CHORUS)

Envelope **28** containing the following letter, postmarked 10 June 1892, Stratford-on-Avon. Holy Trinity Church, where Shakespeare is buried, is pictured.

Temperance Hotel
Stratford
Friday
[10 June 1892]

Dearest Lennie

You probably expected a letter before this, but you know what a worker I am & how seldom I rest from my labours!

I found 12 miles [29] in the sun rather much for my well shod feet – as Homer would say – however I struck the old tram track & strode into Stratford in real Galway style – with shoes & stockings slung over my shoulder. The river looked very gay with all the boats & the town itself seemed to me a pleasant abode. After being here some days I have a growing conviction that a party of the name of Shakespeare once lived in the vicinity, when I go into a shop to buy a penny bun or an envelope I am shown photographs of his birthplace, or told where I can see the toothbrush Mr S used when a boy. As boys seldom use these articles I infer he was something out of the common.

To show their appreciation of the drama, the men of Stratford have built a beautiful theatre. The place would pay, only 'Walker's American Hippodrome' (from Paris) comes along in the height of the season & draws off all the play going public to look at two sea lions & a spotted mule.

Dr Collisson has found a mutual friend who is to interview the manager of the Lyric [30] about Strongbow. I also hear from another source that the Lyric wants a comic opera so we may be millionaires yet. I haven't done as much work as I expected, the sun has been awful & one can do little else besides bathe. I sat out in the sun sketching on Wednesday & it seems to have taken my usual sprightliness from me. Alfred Godley [31] writes to ask us down to Oxford next Tuesday. How does that suit? No bicycle as yet, so I shall probably return tomorrow to Shipston by carrier – 'this side up, with care.' Till then farewell dearest Lennie

ever your devoted

Percy

Watercolour by Percy French 'Boat on River, Warwickshire'.
This is the River Stour, with Lennie and her dog Rex in the boat.

70 Redesdale Street
[July 1892]

Dearest Lennie,

I am just recovering from a wild night round town with Mrs Sheldon. I meant to
have taken her to see 'A Pantomime Rehearsal' **32** but she gave me too short notice & I
could only get a box at the Gaiety. However 'Cinder Ellen' seemed to amuse her though
dear Lottie Collins is indisposed & did not appear. We looked very fine & large in the
stage box & ate ices with elegance & grace between the acts. Tonight we go to see our dear
old friend Toole in 'Walker London' & we hope to have Miss Dorothy B. with us. I called
on that young lady on Monday and found her all that your fancy painted her & not so
dark as somebody photographed her. We went round some of the small galleries & from
the way she picked out the good work I think she promises to be a talented artist. She
spoke very nicely of you dear – but then everyone does – it will get monotonous soon. On
Sunday last Dr C took me to St Matthias', **33** where he is singing in the choir at present.
The 2nd service (I don't know the technical name) rather surprised me. 80 lighted
candles on the altar, procession with candles & incense, bowings & posturings of every
description left me rather at sea. The music compared favourably with Miss Carrie's
efforts – even in her palmiest days. The incensing I failed to grasp the meaning of & I
found myself yawning in the face of a youth who was swinging a censor in my direction.
The Doctor and I afterwards took a sixpenny steamer trip to Kew where we ate buns &
admired the gardens & the river immensely. I am going there again next Saturday to
sketch & have asked Miss Dorothy to come with me, if she can get away from her class. I
hope you are having a good rest & that my brawny arms will find you less of a feather
weight next time I carry my Lennie in them. I met 'Paul' who is also called 'Pauly' at the
Great Western **34** yesterday. He seemed a nice fellow but very quiet & reserved. I am to
meet D'Oyly Carte at 2oc. on Friday next, but cannot say what will come of it, something
for our mutual advantage let us hope. And now goodbye sweetheart goodbye

> ever darling your
> loving
> Percy

I don't think I shall go to Ireland before August. What about a few days in Burmington on
your centenary which takes place end of July I think. **35**

Signed postcard of Houston Collisson.[36]

My darling Lennie

     I put off writing several days in hopes I should be able to tell you some good news of my interview with D'Oyly Carte but alas after footering around the Savoy for several hours we only saw the manager who informed us that Mr Carte would write to us concerning Strongbow. He wrote next day to say he couldn't give us a hearing, as he was very pressed for time – hinc ilae lacrymae – which is Latin. However I have found two mutual friends who know Sedger [37] of the Lyric so all may yet be well. I saw Hamlet for the first time last night – it is not as funny as 'Love All' but the scenery & staging were splendid. A man who has a knowledge of D'Oyly Carte told me today that I would have a better chance there with a libretto without music written to it, as Soloman Sullivan & Slaughter are the popular musicians just now. Dr C [38] approves of 'Love All' & between us we have knocked up some good ideas. We are booked for Horse Show Week & hope to lure the unwary public into our toils. I am not honouring Dublin with my presence this week, but am looking forward with great delight to your coming of age on the 31st. Did I tell you about the service at St Mathias' – great skillets! – we went to Westminster Abbey on Sunday afternoon which I liked better. The organ, choir & sermon (Canon Farrar [39]) were all quite up to the Burmington standard – if not beyond it. I write this at the G. W. Hotel en route for Lynmouth & as my train will soon be off I post this here & will send another instalment from Taunton. I have been a little depressed lately & this is not a very lively letter still

       darling Lennie I
       am happy when
       I think you are
       growing to love me
         ever your
           Percy

The Great Western Hotel, Paddington.

"Who's to win her?"
~~act humour~~ or song
Scene a studio.
_____

(Students chorus as curtain rises
Larry & ~~Bella~~ ^{Rose} both in excentric
carnival costumes discovered
dancing polka. Sandy Mc art at
easil painting the face of a baboon
to the music)

<u>Rose</u>. Oh Sandy I danced every
dance! I ~~must~~ go & make
myself some coffee
(~~exit Rose~~)

<u>L.</u> Can I help you Rose

<u>R.</u> No Larry thank you.
(exit Rose)

<u>S.</u> So the fancy dance was a
great success Larry.

<u>L.</u> not a great success Sandy, ^{sure} I only
~~danced~~ three times with Rose

Trial sketches.

Envelope containing the following letter, postmarked 26 July 1892, Lynmouth.
Note the stamp as flag, and the hand inscribing the address in the sand.[40]

Lynmouth
Monday 25 July [1892]

Dearest Lennie

You will see I am still here, but I take flight tonight for Minehead & thence to Wantage. I thought it better for me morally & physically to dwell rather in the sylvan dales of well wooded Lynn than amid the garish splendours of 70 Redesdale Street, Chelsea. I meant to stay here till Wednesday but I find it takes from 6 in the morning to 6.30 at night to get to Letcombe Regis from here so I am going part of the way this evening per bicycle. I have a large collection of sketches most of them improvements on all previous efforts which is satisfactory. I hope to see the mosques and minarets of Shipston on Friday next, as I suppose the Bairds [41] will require two whole days to know & appreciate me. I suppose Mr Sheldon has drawn out a Home Rule bill by this time. So long as people come in their thousands to see 'Love All' I don't care who is in or out. The Election Skit is 'Off' as I couldn't make much out of it, but I am working up an artistic skit which I think will go, making a good deal of the remarks the children make when the landscape painter is at work. Just got a small cheque from Francis & Day, [42] royalty on a song of mine. I indulged in 4 d. of gooseberries in consequence of this sudden access of wealth. As I don't return to London my birthday presents to you (which were to have been numerous & costly) will probably have to be postponed for a week or so, however Aunt Grace will probably put me on the track of something suitable for an elderly maiden lady with a taste for beer, music, big dogs, & bees. This being my last day here I must run off & sketch so send a line to the chalet
        to your
                loving
                        Percy

[July 1892]

Darling Lennie,

Here I am steaming out of Paddington with a mob of flannel clad Henleyites. [43]
The Dr and I thought of going there yesterday but when we found it was 8/- [44] return
(not including boat or grandstand) we stayed in London & bought a lb. of strawberries
instead, the first strawberries are to be had in Chelsea just now at 2d. a lb.! A conservative
of the name of Whitmore got in for Chelsea [45] - but tell your father I had nothing
whatever to do with it, the Primrose League are to blame - not me. I took Dorothy B &
a young friend of hers to Richter's [46] concert last Monday & they both were delighted,
D told me she had never heard music before. Under the Dr's tuition we are becoming
advanced Wagnerites. He and I went to Moore & Burgess [47] the night after & came away
sadder & wiser men. I see Godley's poems reviewed in the Pall Mall, [48] they call them
clever but only to be understood of Oxford men. Remember me to Mr & Mrs S.
I miss the latter in my midnight frolics about town. Also kind regards to Miss Lindé.
I suppose you give guitar lessons now. I enclose 2 strings in case of accidents.
What about that photograph. I am sending you a book by Daudet but don't be frightened -
my family have read it which makes it eminently respectable, your loving

Percy

Alfred Godley.

Alfred Godley became Public Orator at Oxford University and also wrote books and comic verses. His best known is below, written on the occasion of the coming of the motorized bus to Oxford in 1914. Latin was compulsory for students for university entrance, and Latin primers were in common use, with the declensions of nouns printed out. Brought up with French's play on words, Godley here declines the English words 'motor' and 'bus' as though they were Latin, not merely derived from Latin. A full explanation is given in the endnotes.[49]

> What is this that roareth thus?
> Can it be a Motor Bus?
> Yes, the smell and hideous hum
> Indicat Motorem Bum!
> Implet in the Corn and High
> Terror me Motoris Bi:
> Bo Motori clamitabo
> Ne Motore caedar a Bo---
> Dative be or Ablative
> So thou only let us live:---
> Whither shall thy victims flee?
> Spare us, spare us, Motor Be!
> Thus I sang; and still anigh
> Came in hordes Motores Bi,
> Et complebat omne forum
> Copia Motorum Borum.
> How shall wretches live like us
> Cincti Bis Motoribus?
> Domine, defende nos
> Contra hos Motores Bos!

29

My darling Lennie

The photographs were received in Lynmouth with much public & private rejoicings. They are like you but not good looking enough – however I know how vain & giddy you are so I forbore to flatter. I find myself much 'fitter' here than in London so am more cheerful & have got a good deal of work done, both writing & painting. About my movements – I go to Dublin after I leave Burmington & stay till almost the end of August. I think Horse Show Week [50] begins about the 21st. Could the Baird family [51] come 'Come Bairdie come' in September? the autumn is the time for sketching in the country everything is too green just now. Well, after the Richter concert the Dr & I tried the Moore & Burgess Minstrels but found them very doleful. After that we surveyed Beerbohm Tree's [52] 'Hamlet' from the gods – a fine performance & the scenery & dresses made our mouths water. Next day I started for Lynmouth but only got as far as Minehead of which unfashionable resort I took a sketch & lodged at a rustic inn. My bill for tea, bed & breakfast was 2/6 which the landlady said as she handed it to me was 'cheap enough God knows'. I suppose she expected me to try & beat down this exorbitant charge & seemed disappointed when I paid her with alacrity – she is no doubt lamenting not having put in a few extras. I cycled to Lynmouth over some appalling hills but getting a fine view of Exmoor – (have you read 'Lorna Doone'? [53] the shops here seem to sell no other book) & after 22 miles suddenly dipping down into Lynmouth. It is a quaint old fishing village but they are beginning to spoil it with slated lodging houses in neat rows instead of the irregular thatched cottages which artists come to sketch. I have a room in one of the latter & am making a picture of it for your edification. There are flocks of lady artists in every corner & a few indifferent males. They generally have some R.A.s [54] down but they don't come till the autumn. I was shown a place on the Lynn yesterday which 'a gent of the name of Millais [55] used to paint.' The old man who pointed it out said he'd heard tell that Mr Millais 'had done well at the business.' I found everyone greatly excited about an election here. I kept my head however & only remarked 'How nice' when told that the Liberal candidate was in by 200 votes!! There is only one tune sung or whistled here and that is 'Ta ra ra boom! de ay' [56] there never was such a craze. My life here is a simple & inexpensive one. Sketching by day, writing at night, an occasional meal & a sound sleep is the record of my existence so there isn't very much to write about. I have to work up a new sketch to follow 'Love All', something in the Corney Grain line. I am thinking of some election skit – 'How I stood for Ballyhooly' but haven't worked it out yet, so if you hear anything comic in the canvassing or election speech line let me have it. I find your paint box a great boon & ascribe some of my best effects to the colours there in. My own little one I gave to Dorothy as I found her working with 'Rowney's unrivalled 1/– paint box for juveniles', price for cash 10d. I suppose Mr Sheldon is chortling over the elections – The grand old man (sic) ought to make him Chancellor of the Exchequer or Warden of the Cinq Ports after all his exertions. I think I shall stay here for another week, then back to London to see if any of the librettos sown in June have born fruit. After that hey! for Burmington & my darling Lennie

     ever your loving

     Percy

Lynmouth Harbour.

act I

Harry.	**Ah, the letters. Any more calls to-night, Larry?**
Larry.	No, sir. I'll be getting home now, sir.
	(Takes out letter and hands it to Harry.)
Harry.	Not before you get your supper, Larry.
Larry.	Thank your honour. Indeed the family was always good to the poor.

(Leaves down letter.)

(Enter Miss Kitty Fitzgerald,-an heiress with a turn for sport

----

Mrs. Clancy.	I can't get this to meet within a fut, master Harry.
Harry.	Oh that's all right; it's a man we're deceiving, he'll think it's an old fashion revived.
Mrs Clancy.	I'll have to wear a cape round me neck wid this fashion.
Harry.	Tom McGurk, what will you do?
Tom.	I help in the yard, sir,-sort o' general man, sir.
Harry.	Just so; you are General Mensergh of the Tipperary Indis- pensibles, you must say"the devil" and "curse me" whenever you speak.
	(Enter the Wren Boys led by Black Dan.)
Dan.	Good night Mr Harry, and thank you kindly.

Dan.	We would, sir.
Harry.	YOU will.

More trial sketches.

Lynmouth
Thursday
[July 1892]

Darling Lennie

Just a line to say I am alive & kicking. Kicking just now because some wealthy Americans have taken the rest of the house I lodge in so I have to leave my front bedroom ('with ample sea view') & retire to a back one with a blank wall within four feet of the window. However I was warned that if the house was taken I should have to be sent to the small profits chamber (joke — ha! ha!) & as I am out all day I don't complain much. This is the Foresters' Fete day so flags are flying everywhere. Up to the present 'the Foresters' seem to consist of a couple of wagonettes full of dusty men & women & a sprinkling of drums — however they will probably develop later on. I don't know anything about this sect but I suppose like the caterpillar 'it was created for some good purpose.' By the way what sect _is_ a caterpillar? The answer to this riddle, which is worthy of Mr Sheldon, will be forwarded on the receipt of 4 stamps. I hear you are looking & feeling better, which I am very glad of & expect to see a combination of Mary Anderson [57] & Mrs Langtry [58] when I arrive at Burmington. Let us have a quiet little time to ourselves & don't make a point of having Mrs Espinasse [59] to dinner — at least not every day. I shall arrive by the 2.20. Programme for the day

> Arrival of W.P.F. at station
> Presentation of ticket (last year's) to Head Porter
> Welcoming address by J Kindred Esq
> Bicycle procession to Burmington
> Reception on steps by household
> Drawing room reception by Miss Sheldon
> LUNCHEON
> 3.30 — 4
> Organ recital by Miss Carrie
> The rest is
>   LENNIE!!!

Mrs Baird — 'Aunt Grace' has asked me to look in at Wantage en route so I shall probably stay here sketching & writing till the 28th & spend a day there as I don't think I can possibly be back at Burmington in August. This is a short little letter dear but one day is very like another here so I don't find much to tell you.

Ever
    your loving
        Percy

Watercolour by Percy French of the millrace at Burmington.
The summer house is still there, at the end of the garden of Burmington House.

4 Herbert Place
Dublin
Saturday
[August? 1892]

Dearest Lennie

If you find my memory knocking about Burmington please forward. I suppose the effort to write songs & sketches between the pauses of the engine was too much for me for I got into a most forgetful state, & began shedding luggage all along the line. First of all I forgot my bag at Moreton & as it contained 'Love All' I had to wait for it at Worcester thereby losing the Burmington train. I toured round Worcester on the bicycle & during my peregrinations lost the copy book containing the rough draft of Miss Dubedat's song & the Lambkin duet out of my side pocket.

Getting back to the station I found my bag had arrived so thought I had better start as soon as possible. I had just time to wire to the Dr not to expect me till Friday morning, & when I got into the train I found I had left an A.B.C. guide & 'Snap shots' on the telegraph counter, after which I felt that I ought to label myself 'returned empties' and go in the guards van. However I got as far as Wolverhampton without loss, this made me overconfident but as I would have forgotten my bag again only that a passenger handed it out to me I saw that my memory was still absent so tied my belongings to the bicycle & had them labelled 'Dublin.' I managed to get some writing done on the boat, but found the Dr was still away at Southsea when I arrived. I saw Sinclair **60** today & he seems to think well of the piece, but is afraid Gunn will not allow us to play it. You know he stopped the Masons theatricals at the Bazaar, he has the patent rights I believe. If this play doesn't come off I shall go on another short sketching tour as the great Williams who saw some of my work today says I am 'getting a howlt of it.' I also saw Mecredy who gratified me with the news that the I. Cyclist circulation had gone down since I stopped writing so I am going to start my waggeries **61** again on a cash down system. No luggage as yet, but as all fashionable friends are away at 'the salt wather' it doesn't matter, & now goodbye dear Lennie, take a rest & get strong. I fear I tire you mentally & physically sometimes, so take advantage of my absence to become 'the strong Woman of Warwick.'

ever your

loving Willie

The Mall **62**
Baldoyle
Nr Dublin
[August 1892]

Dearest Lennie

Here I am on the margin of the far resounding sea once more. I have taken a room here for a week & am studying sand and seaweed with such success that already the local policeman thinks very highly of my work.

This is a wonderful place for skies – I thought I had finished painting at 9 oc. last night when up rose the moon & began casting reflexions & dodging behind clouds in full view of my window so I had to try & imitate her performance on paper.

Your idea of my returning to Burmington at once is a most brilliant one and at any other time I would return like the prodigal son – dove – moth or boomerang (metaphors selected while you wait) but this place just now is the chance of a lifetime & I feel I am leaving all previous efforts far behind. Thank Mrs Sheldon for her offer to put up with me so soon after my last visit & don't imagine it is any disinclination on my part which prevents me recoiling like an indiarubber spring (more metaphors) upon you. The sketching club exh. opens in Oct. & Orpen **63** & I will want about 80 pictures apiece for our own show so I find 3 acres of sand & a seagull a fine way of filling up space. 'Love All' has been knocked about by our stage manager & is beginning to read very well. It is booked for 6th Oct. Do you want another book for the reading society yet? I will stay here about 10 days & then hey! per 'The Sheldon Arms' & the fleshpots of Burmington House. I enclose a note from my mother which came in her last letter also a cutting from the Cyclist **64** with Will Wagtale's last: not much of an effort but the Ed. had nothing for me to write about so I had to knock off something with the (printer's) devil at my elbow. I find my tennis has improved! so those games with you didn't do me the harm you anticipated. I hope you & Mrs Espinasse are having some singles. Have you ever used the sketch box? if not I shall regret not having carried it off. And now goodbye dear – it is <u>not</u> just past time, but it's time to think of some topic for the Cyclist & a song for 'Love All'. With love to you & kind regards to the livestock. I am ever your

loving Percy

The Mall, Baldoyle, in 2014.

The Irish Cyclist, 10 August 1892:

Will Wagtale has returned to Dublin, to the joy of his friends and creditors.
(Daily paper).

'Oh, William the Wagglesome, where have you been,
   And what have you been about?'
'I've been to London to visit the Queen,
   But the parlour-maid said she was "Hout"
And the Editor smiled with a smile serene,
   And calmly replied, 'No doubt.'

'Oh, William the Wagglesome, what have you done,
   And what have you heard that's new?'
'I've cycled with luggage that weighed a ton,
   And the front fork's all askew.
I know I'm an ass and you think me one,'
   And the Editor said, 'I do.'

'Oh, William the Wagglesome, what is best known,
   The air tyre, cushion, or what?'
'They told me', said William, 'on meeting a stone,
   My tyre would go off like a shot,
And over the hedge I'd be certainly thrown.'
   And the Editor muttered, 'What rot.'

'Oh, William the Wagglesome, whom have you seen?
   Have you met any English fliers?'
'I met two fellows who thought me green —
   They said that on solid tyres
Their one mile record was 2.15,'
   And the Editor murmured, 'Liars.'

'Oh, William the Wagglesome, what did you ride?
   Let's know how the bicycle did?'
'It did very well,' the wag replied —
   'In the luggage compartment hid.'
Then the Editor rising in wrath said 'Glide!'
   So Wagglesome William glid.

WILL WAGTALE

Dearest Lennie

    My cargo of 10 masterpieces has just been sent to Belfast so I am able to lay aside the brush & once more grasp the pen. Affairs re 'Midsummer Madness' are rather mixed as Miss Dubedat **65** *has returned her part saying it doesn't suit her so the Doctor is going to get some lady over from London, perhaps that eminent actress Mddle. Helen Sheldon would like to resume her place on the Irish boards? also Gunn has forbidden any performance except in a licensed theatre. We think of the foyer of the Leinster Hall if we can get it cheap. Little Lord Faultyboy reads very well & should act funnily but the recreant Doctor is afraid of appearing – it is too much of a burlesque – I think personally he is right but he would have looked very comic as His Lordship. The last two 'Cyclists' have had 'pomes' of mine in them. I send on the last in case you didn't see it, Mecredy is very anxious that I should start a serial tale to run thro. the winter months. What about you supplying an intricate plot & sharing the profits!! Just got a letter from Cecilia Countess of Annesley* **66** *wondering what has become of me. A wedding present must go to her at once – at once mind. You would have been amused with my efforts to christen some of my pictures this morning. 'Sunrise at Lynmouth' figures in Belfast as 'The last ray Portmarnock'. The truth is too prosaic for me – 'anybody could do it.' Do you see a likeness between Dorothy's handwriting & the little bit I enclose. I found it wrapped round a tiny purse of coins.*

    This is not a very entertaining epistle I fear but I have done nothing but paint, not even been at the bank to have a chat tho. I was asked several times. With kind regards to all I remain, your loving

    Willie Percy F.

A group including the Count and Countess of Annesley, with French fifth from left in the first standing row and Lennie in the back row, seventh from left. The Countess is holding her first daughter Clare, born June 1893, so the photograph is most likely from 1894.

The Irish Cyclist, 17 August 1892:

'A young lady proposes going alone around Ireland on a bicycle.'

'Wagtale,' said the rejuvenescent editor of the I.C. handing me the above par, 'there's a subject for verse, eh?'

'Thomas Moore would be the best man to tackle such a theme,' replied I, with that becoming modesty which is three parts laziness and one ignorance.

'Then ring up Thomas Moore, if he is *the* better man — we want no expense spared to make this paper the cycling paper of the solar system!'

The telephonic answer was to the effect that Moore had died long ago and left no address (I may mention parenthetically that unless a man is a racing cyclist we know nothing about him in *this* office). So after a draught from the Pierian spring of one Kop's, I threw off my coat and these talented verses:

Stitched with care was the dress she wore, [67]
And a bovril drop in her hand she bore,
But, oh, her cycle was just a shade
In front of her clothing — tho' tailor made.

'Lady, dost thou not fear to scoot
All unprotected along the route;
Are Erin's sons and her daughters, too,
Not likely to make it too hot for you?'

'Sir Knight, I feel not the least alarm,
I have what is known as a personal charm;
And if anyone harbour a thought of guile,
I disarm them — thus — with my maiden smile.'

On she went, but her maiden smile
Changed to a frown in a little while;
For Erins' sons were extremely rude,
And Erin's daughters came out and 'booed.'

Still she pedalled — mid urchins' yell,
And squeaky orders to 'ring the bell;'
But missed the road ere she came to Bray,
So returned that evening another way.

WILL WAGTALE

The Irish Cyclist, 24 August 1892:

WILL WAGTALE AGAIN!

We wrote last week to that old reprobate, Will Wagtale, for a soul-stirring contribution to our current issue, and here is his reply.

The Mall, Baldoyle.

MORE THAN EVER RESPECTED SIR! — You have come back to your native soil — Napoleon is once more among his eagles — the prodigal has returned, and 'fatted calf and potatoes for one' is being served in Rockville's pillared Fane.

Though I am of a literary turn I have not been reading your valuable paper lately, so I have no idea what you have won. I have yet to read, with beating heart, how you looked and what you wore, but I trust you retained the spectacles and the winning smile which have endeared you to the caricaturist. I would have waited upon you (about lunch hour) yesterday, but my creditors are on the alert, and only an old address and a pneumatic keep them off the scent.

I have been in the neighbourhood of Baldoyle for the last ten days making a full length portrait — nearly life size — of the Hill of Howth.

Whilst sketching on the sands I have had an opportunity of watching the sweet little children at play. I am going to start a branch of the S.P.C.C., called the 'Society for the Prevention of Cruelty *in* Children.' I am quite aware that a crab can grow a new pair of legs or an improved nipper whenever he has the misfortune to lose one or other of these appendages. Still it must be very annoying to an elderly crustacean hurrying along to business (a trifle late, maybe, owing to not having been called in time) to have his legs pulled off by a dear little child. I notice a growing want of cordiality in the attitude of crabs towards children — and no wonder.

On Saturday I went on what for me was rather an extended cycle tour — about five miles and a bit — round Howth Head. The ladies' bathing place seems to be a subject of contemplation for Howthites, and as I paused in my ascent to gaze down upon the sirens disporting themselves in the waves below, the words of Mrs Barrett Browning's beautiful song came forcibly to my mind:

> Have you seen the ladies bathing, oh, my brothers,
>
> Have you seen the bathers bobbing in the sun?
>
> Some are slender, but, by Jingo, there are others
>
> Who weigh at least a ton!

Certainly dress does make a difference — also the want of it.

The first thing I do on one of my cycle tours is to look for a nice safe place where I can stow away my bicycle; you thus have it handy when you come back, and are not bothered with it on your journey. However, my object in writing is not to give you hints on cycle tours, but to advise you to lead forth the Ohne Hast for a day's racing on the 'velvet strand' at Portmarnock. I had a seagull there as pacemaker when I was there yesterday, and we fairly flew — at least he did. — Yours loquaciously,

W. WAGTALE

From *The Irish Cyclist*, showing French as Will Wagtale [sic], top right.
R.J. Mecredy is at lower left. Illustration by Richard Orpen.

The Irish Cyclist, 19 October 1892:

Will Wagtale's biography having appeared in the latest edition of the 'Poets of Ireland,' he is putting on all sorts of side (suicide is, we regret to say, not among them). His application for the vacant Laureateship has, however, we are glad to say, met with a well-merited rebuff from headquarters.

His letter of application, enclosing samples, was returned to this office yesterday. We print it as a warning to other aspirants (with the accent on the ass).

The Cock-loft, Baldoyle.

To Her High and Mightyness Queen Victoria.

RESPECTED MAM,

Having seen in a copy of the *Weekly Freeman* (lent me by my landlady) that the post of Laureateship was vacant, I beg to state that, in my humble opinion, I am the boy for the place.

I don't know if you take in the IRISH CYCLIST, or if you see it at the particular news-room which you frequent. In either case you will be well acquainted with my poetry. However, in case you may have mixed me up with Graphis or Philander, I enclose a few samples which, I think, ought to prove my fitness for the situation. I don't know if the office includes residence, or if the spare bedroom at Windsor has a fireplace, but these are matters that could be arranged when we meet.

I meant to have got the letter type-written for you, as I hear you have to wear specs, but they wanted 2/- for doing it, and you know yourself how many a little thing 2/- will buy for the house coming on Christmas. R.J. Mecredy (of Mecredy & Kyle, see Trade Directory) will testify to my promptness in turning out verse, and applying for my salary.

I saw something of your eldest son when he was over here, and would like to have seen more of him, but I had only a bob ticket and he was in the grand stand among all the nobs.

You probably wouldn't remember me if you saw me, though I waved my hat to you from the top of a Brompton Bus as you passed out of Hyde Park last summer.

Hoping you and the family are all quite well,

I remain,
Yours hilariously,
W. WAGTALE

P.S. — I enclose a stamped and directed envelope, so all you have to do is to write your answer inside and post at the nearest pillar-box.

W.W.

The Irish Cyclist, 12 October 1892:

ADVENTURES OF MR. HARVEST HOLMES.

By Monan Toil.

I had invited Holmes to Ireland, and after sitting up all night to consider the matter, he accepted my invitation, appearing abruptly the following evening at my rooms in 'The Cock-loft,' Baldoyle.

He had grown older since I last saw him. Few men leading his life could have done otherwise, but I soon saw that his powers as a li — his literary value, was unimpaired.

He had brought no luggage except his violin-case, a microscope, and that imperturbable look which his friends were getting a little tired of.

It did not take long to make him feel at home; he had a knack of appearing to have lived in any place he happened to drop into for years, and as he lay back in the only armchair, my slippers on his feet, and my unfinished cigar between his lips, he might have been the proprietor, instead of a guest who had arrived five minutes previously.

I was about to tell him something of what was to be seen in the neighbourhood, but he rather impatiently requested me to hold my tongue.

'My good fellow,' he said. 'I have already mastered the contents of Mecredy's road book and map, so am in a postion to teach *you*; pass the sherry, and for heaven's sake shut up.'

After this I thought it better to sit at his feet — a position, indeed, which I was compelled to assume, as he monopolised the only chair — and imbibe instruction from his lips.

'There will be a crime committed shortly,' remarked Holmes, lighting a fresh cigar, 'and the victim will come to consult me.'

I stared at him in astonishment.'How do you know?' I said.

'Pooh!' he replied, 'nothing easier. There is no moon, consequently the night is dark. You follow me so far?'

I nodded.

'Then, as any Englishman will tell you, crimes are of constant occurrence in Ireland, and lastly — your editor wants copy — *voila tout!*'

'But,' I objected, 'why should the victim of the robbery or assault or whatever it is, come to you in preference to the police?'

'He will be searching for the police barracks, which I observed are next door, but in his dazed condition, he will most likely knock at the wrong house; consequently, as I said, he will come here. Ah! there he is.'

There was a hasty knock at the door as he spoke; impelled by an ungovernable curiosity I bounded from my seat on the floor and rushed to admit our visitor.

An elderly man in a very dishevelled condition, and carrying several parcels, stood on the doorstep.

'Is this the police barrack?' he asked.

'Come in,' shouted Holmes, who had remained by the fire; 'take a seat,' he added, pointing to the coal scuttle. 'And now, sir, what can we do for you?'

'I must first tell you who I am —'

'Quite unnecessary,' interrupted Holmes, yawning. 'You are a married man stopping in Baldoyle for the summer. You have been in Dublin shopping, and having had several commissions to execute for your wife at the stores, you were unable to get back till the late train. On your way from the station, you were assaulted and knocked down by a ruffian, who, observing the abnormal thickness of your head, struck you with some blunt instrument across the legs, and then finding that you were neither killed nor disabled, made off without robbing you. Your first impulse was to follow and make faces at your assailant, but the darkness of the night warned you that this would have little effect. You, therefore, proceeded to inform the police, and here you are.'

'Are you the district inspector?' asked the stranger, 'because if so all I want —'

'Pardon me,' said Holmes; 'you evidently have not heard of me; you don't take in 'The Strand.'

'Some of it,' interjected our visitor, dusting his trousers.

'I mean, you have never heard of Holmes, the detective, who, from his skill in dogging criminals, is now known as "Dogs Holmes?" '

'Never, and all I want —'

'Pardon me; all you want now is to find the criminal, and that is my province. Allow me to examine you through this miccroscope. Ah, as I expected, there are particles of sand — you have been "sand-bagged." Please don't interrupt; the sand-bag is a weapon only used among the French convicts in the hulks at Toulon. It is as effective as a bludgeon, and has the advantage of leaving no mark upon the skin; consequently, your assailant was a Frenchman over here for his health, though not for yours.'

'All this is tommy rot — what I want is —'

'To find the criminal — quite so; but we must proceed cautiously. We must not alarm our bird; he is most likely in hiding at this moment in the marshes of Portmarnock, or the rocky fastnesses of Sutton.'

'Bosh,' shouted the stranger. 'He's at home at his tea, and I know him.'

Holmes' face fell. 'You know him,' he said, blankly.

'Yes,' he's a young jackass named Smith, and goes charging about on his bicycle at night. I told him next time he ran into me I'd summons him. *Is* this the police barrack?'

'No,' said Holmes, softly, 'it's next door.' Then, when we were once more alone, he murmured: 'I wish these Irish cyclists carried lamps.'

W. WAGTALE

LEINSTER HALL (FOYER),

MR. W PERCY FRENCH and DR. W HOUSTON COLLISSON

Have the honour to announce that they have made arrangements with Mr. Michael Gunn to transform the Foyer of the Leinster Hall into a Bijou Theatre for the production of their " Triple Bill," which will be produced on MONDAY, OCTOBER 31, & following Nights. At Eight o'clock.

The Performance will commence with a Burlesque Episode, in One Tableau, entitled :—

LITTLE LORD FAULTYBOY

BY W. PERCY FRENCH.

Scene : Morning Room in Town House of Lord Dormouse.

Illustrations.

Lord Dormouse	MR. W. THOMAS
Little Lord Faultyboy	DR. W. H. COLLISSON
Mrs. Errol	MISS ALICE LINDE
Mrs. O'Pake	MISS DUBEDAT

To be followed by an Entirely New and Original Sketch entitled :—

SNOOPING !

Or, Reminiscences of a Sketching Tour.

BY W. PERCY FRENCH.

To conclude with an entirely New and Original Operetta, entitled :—

MIDSUMMER MADNESS

Written by w. PERCY FRENCH. Music by w. HOUSTON COLLISSON

Tableau I. - Morning. Tableau II. - Evening.

Illustrations.

Captain Mackintosh	MR. W. S. NORTH
Rev. Mr. Jones (a Photographic Enthusiast)	MR. W. H. SINCLAIR
Grogson (the Family Butcher)	MR. W. THOMAS
Lady Betty	MISS ALICE LINDE
Rose	MISS DUBEDAT

Production under the direction of MR. W. H. SINCLAIR

SPECIAL SCENERY PAINTED BY MESSRS. G. A. JACKSON AND CECIL HICKS, GAIETY THEATRE.

PRICES OF ADMISSION :—Reserved Seats (numbered), 3s.

Admission, ONE SHILLING.

Plan of the Hall may be seen and places secured at the booking Offices of Messrs. PIGOTT & Co., 112 Grafton Street, and of Messrs. CRAMER, WOOD & Co., 5, Westmoreland Street. Places should be secured immediately.

MECREDY & KYLE, PRINTERS, 49, MIDDLE ABBEY STREET, DUBLIN. 3394.

Triple Bill.

A selection of reviews.

The Lady (Nov. 1892):

Triple bills seem quite the fashion... and at the Leinster Hall Dr Houston Collisson and Mr French had their variety entertainment running for a fortnight - a burlesque on 'Little Lord Fauntleroy,' with the author dressed so as to represent the youthful lord; then followed a capital sketch by Mr French, entitled 'Snooping,' followed by a little operetta, 'Midsummer Madness,' well written and played, the leading stars being Miss Du Bedat and Miss Alyce Lindé.

Daily Independent (1 Nov. 1892):

Mr French's sketch [Snooping] is full of clever things, one of the best being the song 'Mat Hannigan's Aunt' which the author renders in fetching fashion, accompanying himself the while on the banjo.

The concluding item of the 'Triple Bill' is a new and original operetta entitled 'Midsummer Madness.' Again is French found in his best form, and he finds a worthy collaborateur in Collisson.

Herald (1 Nov. 1892):

Mr French contributed, besides the words of 'Midsummer Madness' and 'Little Lord Faulty Boy', a very funny sketch of the difficulties and dangers that beset the artist on a sketching tour. 'Snooping' - if you want to know what it is consult Mr French - is genuinely amusing.

Evening Telegraph (1 Nov. 1892):

. . . the skit is undoubtedly an amusing one. The ease and self-confidence with which Dr W.H. Collisson donned the velvet tunic and lace of 'Little Lord Faultyboy' proves that the 'popular concert' organizer has developed a new talent, and his acting throughout was uncommonly good and at times most entertaining.

Watercolour by Percy French of Rex and the cat in the drawing room at Burmington.
The window is still there in 2015.

[November 1892]

Dearest Lennie

You are very patient with me, for I feel that my conduct is not above reproach. I am booked for a concert on the 14th of Dec. **68** *after which I will run over to Burmington if the Dr doesn't book me for 3 days in Cork, they want us to go there with our 'Triple Bill', but we want higher terms than they will accept I think. I am trying to collect ideas for my show with Orpen, which must come off in January. Pictures selling fairly well, & the critics see a great improvement in my style. 'M.M.'* **69** *was a success & amused all grades of men women & children but dividing with Gunn is not good enough. This is why I want to work up something with Orpen. I will send you a line to tell you how our tour gets on. Belfast Opera is off for the present. I believe the local chorus came to blows.*

Ever yours

Willie

Darling Lennie

I haven't much to tell you of as yet as my time has been taken up in making appointments & trying to finish the plot of Don Quicksett. I lunched with the hospitable Mansergh **70** *yesterday & he and his wife both like the idea of the Don enormously. I got to Moreton at 3 oc. which was good going up hill & against a wind. It was very lucky that I went so fast as I found the train has been altered to 3.5 & only stops at Oxford so I got in to town about 5.20. The guitar wasn't as bad as I expected so I will personally conduct it to Wantage (if we go there, as I hope dearie we will). I have written a diplomatic letter to Sala & enclosed the poem which I hope will fetch him. I went to In Town on Wednesday & saw the Serpentine dancer 'Loie Fuller.'* **71** *She is very nice, but I don't think my mother would approve of her. The piece itself is not strong but is carried off by the acting. I also saw 'Mamzelle M'touche' a comic opera which begins well but dwindles off into 'Victoire' at times. I am studying comic opera at present and have no cause as yet to be ashamed of Strongbow. My other shoe left London on Tuesday last for Burmington so I am still 'on the hop.' Tomorrow I go round interviewing. I have got some flattering introductions, so let us hope Eldorado is on the horizon. Send me a work of art in your latest manner soon.*

I hope by Sunday to have something more definite to tell you, meanwhile keep up your heart and remember you are

> *loved more than ever*
> > *by your*
> > > *wandering sweetheart*
> > > *Willie*

Some pictures that I left at Smiths I find were sent to Burmington. You might return them here as I will go to some picture dealers on Monday.

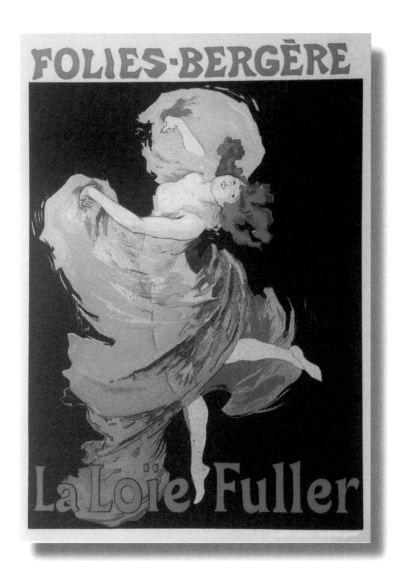

Sunday, 16
[1892]

Darling Lennie

I had a long chat with Graves (sub Ed. of Globe) on Friday. He told me the best thing I could do to get a hold of Editors was to get out a book containing samples of my wares (published at the publisher's risk) & even if my share of profits was nil it would be the quickest way of getting into the groove that suited my style. He happens to know the literary agent who brought out Kipling & Haggard & I go to him tomorrow with a lot of my former works (prose & poetry) which I luckily have with me. I have spent the last two days in knocking it into shape, and done nothing else except see 'The Second Mrs Tanqueray' **72** *a powerful play splendidly acted, of which I will give you a full & partially true account when we find ourselves together — at opposite ends of the room. I had a letter from Aunt Grace asking me down but I think it will be Burmington again as you can't leave I presume. My movements will depend on what the agent says tomorrow. I would like to get up a few more rungs on the ladder of art before I commenced pot boiling. The St James' has not returned my last article 'a brush with the natives' so they may be going to publish it after all. I hear Astor is working the Pall Mall so money is no object. I am going to have a shot at it, I hope you are not considered accountable for the high death rate among the ducks, kleine Schatz.*

Things are still a little indefinite darling, but I really am trying my best to collect feathers for our little nest. I hope Aunt Bell is better, & not incubating any of our misdemeanours.

So good bye dearie
for a little while
ever your loving
Willie

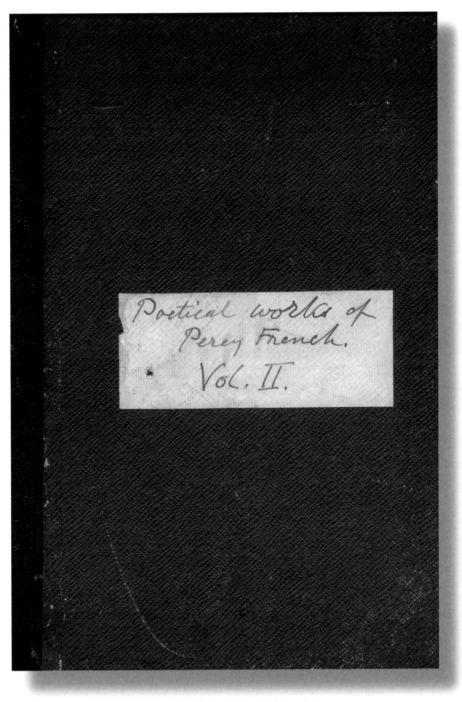

One of French's books of typed samples.

*(insert at * on p.f.? act II)*

Kitty. Ha! what regiment is this?

Dan. We mostly come from Crosmalina.

Kitty. Then the crosmalind regiment
must have its marching song.
Attention! eyes front! chest forward
mouth open! Steady

(act II)

"The Crosmalina Tarriers".

Song. (Kitty Fitzgerald and chorus.)

I.

Kitty. I'll sing about you,

But you first must have a name. *(put all in one line)*

Chorus.A name, a name,

Now what shall be that same?

Kitty ~~The~~ *as* Crosmalina Tarriers.

~~Kitty.~~ I'll have you known to fame.

Chorus.That name, that name,

We'll never, never shame.

Kitty. No one would suspect

That you had been in any war.

It shows what very, very, very, clever men you are.

To go through all this fighting, and come out without a ~~scar~~

Wonderful the boys of Crosmalina.

~~Chorus.~~The Crosmalina Tarriers ~~are terrors at a fight;~~
are terrors at a fight!
They walk through bars and barriers ~~on any moonlight night.~~
On any moonlight night.
They hunt the foe like harriers, ~~and when the evening's~~
And when ~~the foom~~ their foes are slain
The Crosmalina Tarriers ~~slain.~~
Come marching home again
Chorus The Crosmalina Tarriers, ~~come marching home again.~~

~~Chorus. The Crosmalina Tarriers, the terrors at~~ _____

II

Kitty I just remember, though 'twas long, long years ago;

Chorus.Just so, just so, 'twas many years ago;

Kitty. How like a herd of buffaloes you rushed upon the foe.

Chorus.Just so, just so, but what's a buffalo?

Kitty. The peelers run to cover when they hear your marching tune
The militia keep in Barracks or go off in a balloon
No ear can stand the chorus that we sing beneath the moon
Sung by the boys of crosmalina. Chorus &c.

Chorus The Crosmalina Tarriers &c. *(Exit Clarin)*

More trial sketches.

Chelsea
[1892]

Darling Lennie

 I hope to start for Burmington by the 4.45 tomorrow (Saturday) & cycle from Moreton. I must be back here on the 28th as Collisson talks of running over with scores of operas on that date & wants me to meet him. I have met Mascheroni **73** *& he seems very clever & anxious to start so I am thickening up the plot to such an extent that its own mother won't know it. I must skirmish about the town now if I mean to start tomorrow so as I will be with you a few hours after you get this I leave all news until I have you snugly ensconsed in your old quarters. My literary agent hasn't written yet. Success seems to have turned Harmsworth's brain.*

 Ever your

  loving

   Willie

70 Redesdale Street
Chelsea.

Dearest Lennie
        You can't think how
glad I am! — I am
off to shepston by the
10 train tomorrow. I
couldn't stay in London
after getting your dear
letter. I only hope I
wont be incarcerated
as an escaped lunatic
on route — I feel like
one — but it is the
delirium of joy. You
have made me very very

70 Redesdale Street
Chelsea
[1892]

Dearest Lennie

You can't think how glad I am! — I am off to Shipston by the 10 train tomorrow. I _couldn't_ stay in London after getting your dear letter. I only hope I won't be incarcerated as an escaped lunatic en route — I feel like one — but it is the delirium of joy. You have made me very very happy — happier than I ever expected to be again. Oh dear Lennie the thought of your being able to care for me — even a little — has made a man of me again.

Hurrah! Hurrah!

You say in your letter that you are very self contained & reserved. I know the feeling well myself but I also know that in the society of one who loves you it disappears.

I hate to stop here but I have a lot to do & this sudden flight to Shipston must be arranged.

So dearest Lennie goodbye till tomorrow — I could have filled this page with terms of endearment, but though I have thought of them in connection with you for many days, I don't like to startle you with a glimpse of the volcano which I feel raging within me — Oh dear, I really must fly.

Goodbye my love

your devoted Willie

70 Redesdale Str
[January? 1893]

Dearest Lennie

I find I can get my ticket extended to end of this month so I am not leaving here till Saturday morning. You might look up trains from Euston to Banbury via Blisworth for me, a pleasant fireside puzzle for you my young friend. I haven't done much except copy pictures in the National Gallery (Turner's) which have strengthened my painting wonderfully. I made rather a better Emsworth since I've been here so I sent the original to the Shaws, also a bog with which they seem pleased. I got a commission from Aunt Grace to buy a guitar for Dorothy. I have marked one down at a shop near here & am now bargaining à oriental style for it. The way money flies here is most amazing. By the way is my other dress shoe chez vous. I have got a copy of Midsummer Madness from Dublin & was to have shown it to German Reed today, but am writing it up a little. I am getting frightened about the weather, it is sure to rain a lot after this & then my great achievements in the sketching line won't come off!

With kind regards to the father
    I am
        your loving
            Willie

Darling Lennie

Your words of wisdom have gone in at one ear & have not yet gone out at the
other. My writings as you say are my trump cards, so I am sending off a selection to the
Authors' Society reader for advice as to publisher & cost. Meanwhile 'Messrs Orpen &
French at Home' is getting into shape but will not be given to the Public until March 1,
as people will have forgotten that they are in Lent by that time. The 'At Home' card which
Orpen has designed as a circular is a work of art, you will receive one when it is printed.

I haven't got many brilliant ideas yet but by the time I have rewritten the 'book'
it will I think be sufficiently sparkling to keep the audience in a titter with an occasional
guffaw from the gallery.

My songs are up to the present, 'Mat Hannigan's Aunt',[74] 'What will my
grandmother say', 'The humour of the day' (showing how prehistoric man had the same
jokes as we have), 'Douglas Jordan' as sung by Laurence Kellie & words brought up to
date, 'a nigger song' & 'The frock that came over from France' (describing a costume
made of home materials — you might suggest something for this last). Also a topical song.
The first part consists of Mr F at home to his audience, he gives his reasons for the 'at
home', the lights are turned down, 'most of us look so much better in the dark' & some of
the more illustrious guests are announced & appear on the screen. I ask Mr North for a
song & as the symphony is being played two ladies commence to talk & continue till end of
song. I don't like to ask audience guests to sing so sing myself, show my photo book and get
Mr Lefanu to tell an Irish story (the one I sent to the Idler & which they returned saying
they were full for some months but hoped to hear from me again — at present it is with the
Strand. No news of it yet.) I don't know how I wind up Part I, but hope to work up some
surprises — Pt II Orpen appears as an artist with campstool & easel &c only 10 minutes to
do a sketch before train goes. I come in as a farmer (Irish) and interrupt the work. I hear
that a picture may sell for £50 so go off to fetch my young son to get a lesson in painting.
I bring in Orpen's young brother[75] who is a very promising artist tho. only 12 & they
have a race as to who will be finished first. Part III is a short sketch on things dramatic
'Amateur acting & its cure' or some such title introducing a couple of recitations of a
topical song.

That is the 'Show' at present but it has a month to develop. I saw a paragraph yesterday saying that M. Yakobrowsky of the Shaftesbury Theatre wanted a librettist so I sent him 'Strongbow' to show him what Hibernia could do. I have also embarked on a serial for the Irish Cyclist (Miss Gyles supplying the plot), but I don't know if it will turn out above or below the average yet. I met the 'mystic' Yeats **76** *again & was shown his 'Life of Blake' which is to be reviewed by Stead at great length in the next R. of Reviews.*

I am sending you a powerful sketch for your old servant which I think ought to suit her. The Editor of the 'Humour Series' has selected 'The first Lord Liftenant' & a poem called 'By the sea' (with interruptions), for his Irish vol. I hope he will get Orpen to illustrate it but the publishers seem to think him too slapdash an artist & can't understand that a joke should never be painfully worked up.

You might send on the glove, handkerchief & sketch. The picture at Stratford might be sold for what it will fetch & the proceeds given to Miss. L. Sheldon. I am very glad to hear you are looking forward to the future & that it helps to make the present go more happily, these are good omens. I hope the 'old folks' are in good health & that you haven't much nursetending to get through. I would be really glad of a few lines soon, it is a long time since I heard from you — my fault I know, but you see I am not idle. I haven't seen the Smiths yet (very remiss of me). I hear Carrickmacross, a very primitive place, was terrified at Alice's low dress!

And now little girl goodbye

ever your loving

Willie

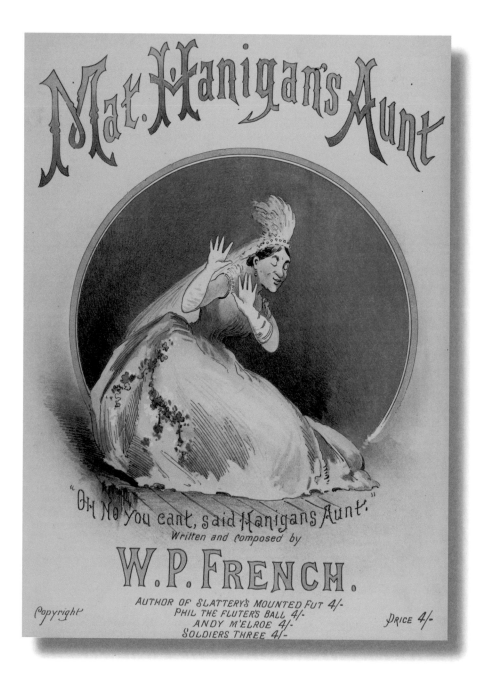

Mat. Hanigan's Aunt

"Oh No you can't, said Hanigans Aunt."

Written and composed by

W. P. FRENCH.

AUTHOR OF SLATTERY'S MOUNTED FUT 4/-
PHIL THE FLUTER'S BALL 4/-
ANDY M'ELROE 4/-
SOLDIERS THREE 4/-

Copyright

Price 4/-

Mathew Hanigan's Aunt.

1.

Oh, Mat Hanigan had an aunt,
    An uncle too likewise;
But in this chant, 'tis Hanigan's aunt
    I mean to eulogize.
For when young lovers came
    And axed her to be their's,
Mat Hanigan's aunt took each gallant
    And fired him down the stairs.

CHORUS.

So here's a health to Hanigan's aunt!
    I'll tell you the reason why,
She always had things dacent
    In the Hanigan family;
A platther and can for every man,
    " What more do the quality want ? "
" You've yer bit and yer sup what's cockin' yees up?'
    Sez Mathew Hanigan's aunt.

2.

Oh, she never could raise her voice,
    She never was known to scold,
But when Hanigan's aunt sed " No, you can't,"
    You did what you were told ;
And if anyone answered back,
    Oh, then his hair she'd comb,
" For all I want," sez Hanigan's aunt,
    " Is peace in our happy home."
        CHORUS.—So here's a health, &c.

3.

Oh, when she went to Court,
    The A-de-congs in vain
Would fume and rant, for Hanigan's Aunt
    Said, " Boy let go me thrain ! "
And when the Lard Liftinant
    A kiss on her brow would imprint,
" Oh no, you can't," said Hanigan's aunt,
    " Widout me pa's consint."
        CHORUS.—So here's a health, &c.

4.

Oh, 'tis often we'd praise her up,
    We'd laud her to the sky,
We'd all discant on Hanigan's aunt,
    And hope she never would die.
But still, I'd like to add—
    If Hanigan isn't about—
That whin we plant Mat Hanigan's aunt,
    We won't be too put out.
        CHORUS.—So here's a health, &c.

Lantern slide by Richard Orpen of Charles II with Nell Gwyn.
In the background is the Royal Hospital, Chelsea, that Charles II founded.

The Mall
Baldoyle
February 1893

Dearest Lennie

I am very sorry I never thought of Valentine's day, sending Valentines has gone out altogether about here, so the shop windows even don't remind you of them. I am quite out of the world here & astonished a man today by not knowing that Parliament were sitting – to say nothing of the Home Rule Bill! What would your father say! The great show is getting into shape, not so many pictures as last time but more (& better) songs.
It will give me quite a new repertoire to 'go to the country' with. My story & Orpen's excellent picture came back from the Strand yesterday — the picture very much damaged which seems rather wanton. However it is off again, this time with an introduction to 'The National Observer' a paper which gives short sketches like the Speaker. Whitbread's benefit comes off soon. I see most of the Strongbow cast down in the bill including Madame Glanville! Miss Madock makes her professional debut at Dr Collisson's benefit next Saturday. I happened to meet one of the Hibernian Academy artists a short time ago & found I had only three days to paint & send in pictures, I had nothing ready, however I set to work & sent in three large works in my most modern manner which I hope to see hung. I have been trying to write a hunting song for the 'At Home.'

Verse 1. Hunting the hare.
   "   2.   "   "   air (orchestral amateurs)
   "   3.   "   "   heir.
   "   4.   "   "   hair (old man)

I will probably sell some of the songs to Pigott [77] afterwards. Arrowsmith wants £35 to publish a collection of my prose & verse. I am getting the Authors' Society opinion on the matter. There is a growing demand for comic (Drawing room) songs, humorous writings & water colours, so I would feel fairly confident if I had this Yeast Co. shares settled. I am trying to get a compromise but I fear it will run off with most of my ready money. Just got a letter from Orpen to say he is out of subjects & is getting anxious so I must stop here & send him something. Very glad you are trying the violin. You ought to play it well, but be careful about how you hold it at the start. It's not a bad fiddle but won't play till it gets to know you.

ever your loving
Willie

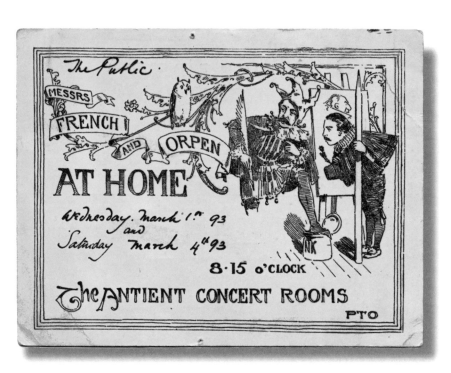

The Public

MESSRS

FRENCH AND ORPEN

AT HOME

Wednesday, March 1ˢᵗ 93
and
Saturday March 4ᵗʰ 93

8·15 o'CLOCK

The ANTIENT CONCERT ROOMS

PTO

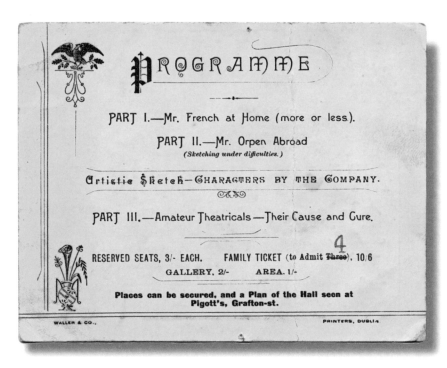

PROGRAMME

PART I.—Mr. French at Home (more or less).

PART II.—Mr. Orpen Abroad
(Sketching under difficulties.)

Artistic Sketch—CHARACTERS BY THE COMPANY.

PART III.—Amateur Theatricals—Their Cause and Cure.

RESERVED SEATS, 3/- EACH.   FAMILY TICKET (to Admit ~~Three~~ 4), 10/6

GALLERY, 2/-   AREA. 1/-

**Places can be secured, and a Plan of the Hall seen at
Pigott's, Grafton-st.**

WALLER & CO.,   PRINTERS, DUBLIN.

Lantern slide by Richard Orpen of the Dublin historian William Lecky.[78]

The Mall
Baldoyle
[March 1893]

Dearest Lennie

The great night is over & though the audiences were very much pleased & went away saying how good it was, the papers have been down on my efforts at entertaining. The I. Times & Express wrote to say their notice was crowded out as there is nothing but 'Home Rule' **79** *in the papers. The other papers go for me which is rather unfair as we kept the house tittering for two hours.*

However we will see what happens on Saturday. The booking is good so far.

I had several new songs which went down very well. 'The Musical revival', 'Hunting the Hare' (air – heir – hair). A serenade (for a tenor & two cats) & a sketch of an amateur play in which the prompter takes the principal part. **80** *I must write to you again tonight as the post is just going, but I know you wanted a line so I send this now. You want some hopeful helpful words, but oh dear I feel rather despondent – I expect the excitement of last week & last night has left me rather limp.*

your loving

Willie

Watercolour by Percy French of part of the garden at Burmington House. The orangery is no longer there.

70 Redesdale Street
Chelsea, London
[1893]

Dearest Lennie

I presume that after our 'good bye at the door' (I saw your last wave from the hill) you are expecting a line as to my fortunes.

Up till now I have done nothing but go round picture galleries & feel like a tourist who has gazed at everything till he is almost cooked (pun). So far my impression is that I have either made a wonderful stride in art or else the Moderns (excepting W.P.F.) have retrograded. I make this statement after mature deliberation so now! Braxton Smith (the man I am stopping with) is related to Dawdswell who has the gallery in Bond Street, & some of my later works (op. cccx) are to be shown to D. on Friday.

Tomorrow I see 'Globe', 'Answers' & 'Up to Date' & try my luck in letters. I don't think I could live in London for long so let me know exact date of our visit southward ho! as I may take a cheap trip 'to Paris & back for 4 days', to see if the Salon is up to the mark.

I hope you are not doing too much – don't run yourself down again. I don't think there is any need for it.

 as I am
  as before
   your loving
    Willie

The First Lord Liftinant

An Historical Sketch
As related by Andrew Geraghty (Philomath).

'Essex,' said Queen Elizabeth, as the two of them sat at breakfast in the back parlour of Buckingham Palace; 'Essex, me haro, I've got a job that I think would suit you. Do you know where Ireland is?'

'I'm no great fist at jografy,' says his Lordship, 'but I know the place you mane. Population, three million; exports, emigrants.'

'Well',' says the Queen, 'I've been reading the Dublin *Evening Mail*, and the *Telegraft*, for some time back, and sorra one o' me can get at the troot o' how things is goin', for the leadin' articles is as contradictory as if they wor husband and wife.'

'That's the way wid papers all the world over,' says Essex. 'Columbus told me it was the same in Amirikay when he was there, abusin' and contradictin' each other at every turn - it's the way they make their livin'. Thrubble you for an egg spoon.'

'It's addled they have me betune them,' says the Queen. 'Not a know I know what's going on. So now what I want you to do is to run over to Ireland, like a good fella, and bring me word how matters stand.'

'Is it me?' says Essex leppin' up off his chair. 'It's not in airnest ye are, ould lady. Sure it's the hoight of the London season. Everyone's in town, and Shake's new fairy piece, 'The Midsummer's Night Mare,' billed for next week.'

'You'll go when yer told,' says the Queen, fixin' him with her eye, 'if you know which side yer bread's buttered on. See here, now,' says she, seein' him chokin' wid vexation and a slice of corned beef, 'you ought to be as pleased as Punch about it, for you'll be at the top of the walk over there as vice-regent representin' me.'

'I ought to have a title or two,' says Essex, pluckin' up a bit. 'His Gloriosity of Great Panjanthrum, or the like o' that.'

'How would 'His Excellency the Lord Lieutenant of Ireland strike you?' says Elizabeth.

'First class,' cries Essex. 'Couldn't be bether; it doesn't mean much, but it's allitherative, and will look well below the number on me hall door.'

Well, boys, it didn't take him long to pack his clothes and start away for the Island o' Saints. It took him a good while to get there though, through not knowing the road; but by means of a pocket compass, and a tip to the steward, he was landed at last contagious to Dalkey Island.

Going up to an ould man who was sitting on a rock he took off his hat, and says he: 'That's grand weather we're havin'?'

'Good enough for the times that's in it,' says the ould man, cockin' one eye at him.

'Any divarshan goin' on? says Essex.

'You're a stranger in these parts, I'm thinkin', 'says the ould man, 'or you'd know this was a "band night" in Dalkey.'

'I wasn't aware of it,' says Essex. 'The fact is,' says he, 'I only landed from England just this minute.'

'Aye,' says the old man bitterly, 'it's little they know about us over there. I'll howld you,' says he, with a slight thrimble in his voice, 'that the Queen herself doesn't know there's to be fireworks in the Sorrento Gardins this night.'

Well, whin Essex heard that he disremembered entirely that he was sent over to Ireland to put down rows and ructions, and haway wid him to see the fun and flirt with all the pretty girls he could find.

And he found plenty of them - thick as bees they were, and each one as beautiful as the day and the morra.

He wrote two letters home next day - one to Queen Elizabeth, and the other to Lord Montaigle, a play-boy like himself.

I'll read you the one to the Queen first.

Dame Street.
April 16, 1599.

Fair Enchantress,

I wish I was back in London, baskin' in your sweet smiles and listenin' to your melodious voice once more. I got the consignment of men and the post office order all right. I was out all morning looking for the inimy, but sorra a taste of Hugh O'Neill or his men can I find. A policeman at the corner of Nassau Street told me they were hiding in Wicklow. So I am making up a party to explore the Dargle on Easther Monda. The girls here are as ugly as sin, and every minite of the day I do be wishing it was your good-looking self I was gazin' at instead of these ignorant scare-crows.

Hoppin' soon to be back in ould England, I remain, your loving subjec,

Essex.

P.S. I hear Hugh O'Neill was seen on the top of the Donnybrook tram yesterday mornin'. If I have any luck the head'll be off him before you get this. - E.

The other letter read this way.

Dear Monty,

This is a great place all out. Come over here if you want fun. Divil such play-boys ever I seen, and the girls - oh, don't be talkin' - 'pon me secret honour you'll see more loveliness at a tay and supper ball in Ra'mines than there is in the whole of England. Tell Ned Spenser to send me a love-song to sing to a young girl who seems taken wid my appearance. Her name's Mary, and she lives in Dunlary, so he oughtent to find it hard.

I hear Hugh O'Neill's a terror, and hits a powerful welt, especially when you're not lookin'. If he tries any of his games on wid me, I'll give him in charge. No brawling for yours truly,

Essex.

Well, me bould Essex stopped for odds of six months in Dublin, purtending to be very busy subjugatin' the country, but all the time only losin' his time and money without doin' a hand's turn, and doin' his best to avoid a ruction with 'Fightin' Hugh.'

If a messenger came in to tell him that O'Neill was campin' out on the North Bull, Essex would up stick and away for Sandycove, where, after draggin' the Forty-foot Hole, he'd write off to Elizabeth, sayin' 'that owing to their superior knowledge of the country, the dastard foe had once more eluded him.'

The Queen got mighty tired of these letters, especially as they always ended with a request to send stamps by return, and told Essex to finish up his business, and not to be makin' a fool of himself.

'Oh, that's the talk, is it?' says Essex. 'Very well, me ould sauce-box' (that was the name he had for her ever since she gev him the clip on the ear for turnin' his back on her). 'Very well, me ould sauce-box,' says he, 'I'll write off to O'Neill this very minit, and tell him to send in his lowest terms for peace at ruling prices.' Well, the treaty was a bit of a one-sided one.

The terms proposed were:

1. Hugh O'Neill to be King of Great Britain.
2. Lord Essex to return to London and remain there as Viceroy of England.
3. The O'Neill family to be supported by Government, with free passes to all theatres and shows of entertainment.
4. The London markets to buy only from Irish dealers.
5. All taxes to be sent in stamped envelope, directed to H. O'Neill, and marked 'private.' Cheques crossed and made payable to H. O'Neill. Terms cash.

Well, if Essex had had the sense to read through this treaty, he'd have seen it was of too graspin' a nature to pass with any sort of a respectable sovereign, but he was that mad that he just stuck the document in the pocket of his pot-metal overcoat, and haway wid him hot foot for England.

'Is the Queen within?' says he to the butler, when he opened the door of the palace. His clothes was that dirty and disorthered wid travellin' all night, and his boots that muddy, that the butler was for not littin' him in at the first go-off. So says he very grand:

'Her Meejisty is abow stairs, and can't bee seen till she's had her brekwish.'

'Tell her the Lord Liftinant of Oirland desires an enterview,' says Essex.

'Oh, beg pardon, me lord,' says the butler, steppin' to one side. 'I didn't know 'twas yourself was in it; come inside, sir; the Queen's in the dhrawin' room.'

Well, Essex leps up the stairs, and into the dhrawin' room wid him, muddy boots and all; but no sight of Elizabeth was to be seen.

'Where's your missus?' says he to one of the maids of honour that was dustin' the chimbleypiece.

'She's not out of her bed yet,' says the maid, with a toss of her head; 'but if you write your message on the slate beyant, I'll see -' but before she had finished, Essex was up the second flight and knockin' at the Queen's bedroom door.

'Is that the hot wather?' says the Queen.

'No, it's me - Essex. Can you see me?'

'Faith, I can't,' says the Queen. 'Howld on till I draw the bed curtains. Come in, now,' says she, 'and say your say, for I can't have you stoppin' long you young Lutharian.'

'Bedad, yer Majesty,' says Essex, droppin' on his knees before her (the delutherer he was), 'small blame to me if I am a Lutharian, for you have a face on you that would charum a bird off a bush.'

'Hold your tongue, you young reprobate,' says the Queen, blushing up to her curl papers wid delight, 'and tell me what improvements you med in Ireland.'

'Faith I taught manners to O'Neill,' cries Essex.

'He had a bad masther then,' says Elizabeth, looking at his dirty boots; 'couldn't you wipe yer feet before ye desthroyed me carpets, young man?'

'Oh, now,' says Essex, 'is it wastin' me time shufflin' about on a mat you'd have me, when I might be gazin' on the loveliest faymale the world ever saw.'

'Well', says the Queen, 'I'll forgive you this time, as you've been so long away, but remimber in future, that Kidderminster isn't oilcloth. Tell me,' says she, 'is Westland Row station [81] finished yet?'

'There's a side wall or two wanted yet, I believe,' says Essex.

'What about the Loop Line,' says she.

'Oh, they're gettin' on with that,' says he, 'only some people think the girders is a disfiguremint to the city.'

'Is there any talk about the esplanade from Sandycove to Dunlary?'

'There's talk about it, but that's all,' says Essex,''twould be an odious fine improvement to house property, and I hope they'll see to it soon.'

'Sorra much you seem to have done beyant spending me men and me money. Let's have a look at that threaty I see stickin' out of your pocket.'

Well, when the Queen read the terms of Hugh O'Neill, she just gave him one look, and jumping from off the bed, put her head out of the window, and called out to the policeman on duty - 'Is the Head below?'

'I'll tell him you want him, ma'am,' says the policeman.

'Do,' says the Queen.

'Hullo,' says she, as a slip of paper dropped out of the dispatches. 'What's this!' "Lines to Mary." Ho! ho! me gay fella, that's what you've been up to, is it?'

> Mrs. Brady's
> A widow lady,
> And she has a charming daughter I adore;
> She's such a darlin'
> She's like a starlin',
> And in love with her I'm getting more and more.
> Her name is Mary,
> She's from Dunlary,
> And her mother keeps a little candy store.

That settles it,' says the Queen, 'it's the gaoler you'll serenade next.'

When Essex heard that, he thrimbled so much that the button of his cuirass shook off and rowled under the dressin' table.

'Arrest that man!' says the Queen when the Head-constable came to the door. 'Arrest that thrater,' says she, 'and never let me set eyes on him again.'

And, indeed, she never did, for soon after that he met with his death from the blow of an axe he got when he was standin' on Tower Hill.

The End

61 Carlisle Mansions
Victoria Road
[1893]

Dearest Lennie

An excellent idea of yours to turn up on Saturday. I will (or shall) probably be at Paddington to see you alight. Have written for tickets for 'Charley's Aunt' **82** *but we will go there whether or no, also do the Academy though it is shorn of its chief glory by the rejection of my turf bank. I wrote to Dorothy on Monday asking her to come that day too so we shall be 'quite a little party'.*

Just off to see Harmsworth — I am still uncertain what to do. I think you might bring the fiddle, if you are on a secure footing with your friends.

Ever your loving

Willie

70 Redesdale Street
[July 1893]

Darlingest of Darlings!

I am wishing you every happiness for your future, rather a selfish wish as your future is my future. I would like to be with you sipping your health in some of that remarkable wine for which your mother is responsible, & afterwards (having had my moustache dried) tasting the lips of my heart's delight.

What good times those were when I had you curled up in my arms. The thought of them makes me wish my Irish tour was over. It's very sweet to think that I can make you happy.

Well to tell you all that has happened since I rode away on my gallant bike. I didn't get to Paddington till 2.15, so found Collisson had gone to the Haymarket leaving however a ticket for me. I found him as large as life in the dress circle. 'A woman of no importance' is chiefly conversational with a couple of dramatic incidents worked in. The cynical Lord Illingworth is a good character ('women are of two kinds – plain & coloured') & an empty headed hostess who put in silly remarks everywhere. ('going out to look at the stars dear? yes we have quite a number opposite our balcony.') Oscar is not up to Pinero by a long way yet. The Dr had to start for Southsea yesterday evg. so after rushing him for ices & buns I saw him off from Victoria. I am not going on tour with him in Ireland which is I think as well & may hasten my return to the arms of my beloved. I found a letter here from Manners asking the price of my <u>bog</u> picture! & also one from Freshwater, from Jubbins, saying two of my pictures were sold the day they arrived (the day he wrote) & to please send more. The two sold were the view from Tennyson's field – an Irish BOG!! The way that treatment of moor takes the public is remarkable! I am sending the photo of Anne Hathaway's cottage to Dorothy to try her luck with. I told her to send her coloured copies to Mr. S & he would leave them at the shop in Stratford. And now about <u>your</u> work 'Geliebtest'.[83] I carried off your last study of leaves & showed it to Miss Barton as <u>mine</u>, she thought '<u>my eye for form & colour had IMPROVED</u>' so now! you see what others see in your work. I went to bed early last night (no theatre) and started 'The Banshee'[84] this morning. I have got on fairly well, up to the entrance of Patsy – his scene with Sir Harry is good, distinctly good – the Don hasn't appeared yet. I think I shall do very little else except write Banshee while I am here, as I take a long time to settle down. Look out for some odds & ends on Tuesday, but my gift won't be very costly, as the minion Collisson, whom I was going to tap for a tenner, begs for time till

Horse Show week when he has taken the Antient Concert Rooms [85] & booked the 'Field Fisher Quartette' [86] & other novelties for the week.

And now my own little girl goodbye, send me a few loving words soon, for I want you ever so much.

your loving Willie

P.S. Let me know when there is another 'fall in eggs' – that is the time to visit the Shelldon's – the (Egg)shelldons – phew (whistle).

CHARACTERS

DR MOULDER   A college Don, (about 50) formerly tutor to
                                Sir Harry Banagher.

SIR HARRY BANAGHER   (of Kilrackety Castle, Co. Galway) about 20
                       in love with Norah Creina.

LARRY McCULL   Postboy, poacher and factotum to Kilrackety.

FRANK FOSBERRY (about 20) just got his commission, in love with
                                Kitty FitzGerald.

CONST. SHEEHAN Of the R.I.C.

DAN JOYCE   "The man who killed Maguire"

LADY BANAGHER   The mother of Sir Harry.

MISS KITTY   Owner of adjoining estate.
FITZGERALD

NORAH CREINA   A foundling.

SMALL PARTS

DR. MACK.   Dispensary Doctor.
MR FEGAN   National Schoolmaster.
PETERS   Butler.
CASEY   An Informer.
MRS CLANCY   Cook.
JOHNNY CUNANE   Fiddler.
TOM   Stable hand. might double with DR.MACK.

POLICE. WREN BOYS. SERVANTS.

List of characters from *The Banshee*.
The full script, as yet unperformed, is in the Castle Museum, Bangor.

The Mall
Baldoyle
[July 1893]

Darling Lennie

　　After a variety of hair breadth escapes I am once more on my native heath.
I found my return tickets from Moreton to Worcester, Worcester to Birmingham & B. to
Stafford were only available for 6 days so I spent a good deal of my time dodging
collectors, with varying success. This left me rather short & I hadn't the price of a cup of
coffee when I got to Chester. However this proved a blessing in disguise, for my more
wealthy travelling companions who got out to refresh were all left behind! We were late
getting into Chester & had to start off again in 4 minutes instead of 10. I knocked up
against the banjo at Holyhead, it was a little the worse for wear but lasted till the last
verse of my last song last night when the tail piece broke in two. The Concert was very
similar to the Burmington Musical festival. 'Hannigan's Aunt' was thought a gem.
We had 'Goodnight' & 'De old banjo' & I see I am to sing in them again at Tallaght
tonight. I have just seen Orpen & we are to set to work tomorrow on our new & original
show. And now dear what are my thoughts since I left you. I think we would be very happy
together & I feel more like work than I have done for some time. I only wish my talents lay
in a more money making groove. The printer & publisher seem to get most of the profit.
Let me have a few lines about yourself soon, your own thoughts would interest me more
than Burmington gossip – which I fear will have to be the subject of conversation at meal
time with you till your poor little head gets addled. We must get to know & help each other
before we start hand in hand 'down the long avenue.' Goodbye sweet heart, don't tire
your industrious little self, as I fear you do too often.

　　ever your loving

　　　　Willie

One of three decorated doors from The Mall, Baldoyle.[87]

Irish Cyclist
[1893]

Dearest little girl,

    A hurried scribble to accompany 'the cycle'. It is a great penny worth though they had several mishaps, for instance the illustrations (some of them) being printed much too small and so are not effective. The photos of the staff also did not come out flattering enough and were condemned as works of art so will have to be done again. However by Xmas time, it and Stead's new paper will we hope be the only two papers in existence.

I write here all the morning and then go out and see pictures. The cycle show every evening and supper afterwards where I enchant the ears of a select gang with song. A good many ladies have taken to cycling in knickerbockers but the broad sleeves kill the effect. It is hard to believe that the female figure is the most beautifully contoured form in nature.

    Don't forget end of Jan '94,

        Your loving

           Willie.

SUPPLEMENT TO THE IRISH CYCLIST, 21ST JUNE 1893

THE "IRISH CYCLIST" STAFF.

H. J. HOLMES (*Philander*).   R. J. MECREDY.   BEATRICE GRIMSHAW (*Graphis*).   A. J. WILSON (*An Old File*).
F. T. BIDLAKE (*Biniljer*).   W. P. FRENCH (*Will Wagtale*).   T. W. MURPHY.

The Irish Cyclist staff, 21 June 1893.[88]

Opposite page, in French's handwriting, reads:

Character of W. P. F. as told by Prof. Annie Oppenheim at Earls Court 1 August 1893.

> A great lover of the beautiful, with a good eye for form & colour. Fond of travel, argumentative but dislikes quarrels & would give up argument with anyone he liked for sake of peace. Heart overrules head. Very sensitive & sympathetic. Resents an injury & rather given to worry over trifles. Great sense of the ludicrous & no reverence. Not vain but glad to be appreciated & knows his own worth, poetical, authoritative but just.

Character of W. P. F.
as told by Prof. Annie
Oppenheim at Earls court
———————— August 1. 93.
A great lover of the
beautiful, with a good
eye for form + colour
Fond of travel, argumentative
but dislikes quarrels & would
give up argument with
anyone he liked for sake of peace
Heart over rules head, very
sensitive. & sympathetic
resents an injury & rather
given to worry over trifles (?)
Great sense of the ludicrous
& no reverence, Not vain
but glad to be appreciated
& knows his own worth,
poetical, authoritative
but just,

Miss A.O.

70 Redesdale Street
Chelsea
[August? 1893]

Dearest Lennie

I got here all safe & with all my parcels including the Cusworth ones. Good old Shaw was lying in wait for the train & came kurrooshing down the platform waving a coat in one hand & a picture in the other. I have been showing my wares to the art dealers & find them inclined to buy. 'The breaking wave' & the 'moorland' are my trump cards everywhere & I could actually do fairly well making copies of my 'bog' for the trade only I feel that I ought to be sketching from nature all this summer & at the rate I am progressing could command twice the price in the autumn, besides winter is the time for studio work. What do you think kleine Schatz?

I interviewed Miss Skidmore this evg. & she seems taken with my poetic feeling for landscape, but thought painting ought to lie, supplemented by other irons. I am to meet her at the private view of the Dudley Gallery [89] next Saturday. I took Dorothy to the water colour institute & also to a morning performance at German Reeds. [90] I haven't been going to any theatres yet but will later. I hope you are not doing too much. I heard yesterday that the Isle of Wight in hot weather was very relaxing so you had better 'lay low' like Brer Fox & get strong. Remember me to your father, Rex, & the rest of the livestock.

Ever
    your loving

      Willie

am to confer with Graves tomorrow.

Watercolour by Percy French, 'The Grey Wolf Wave of Dawn'.

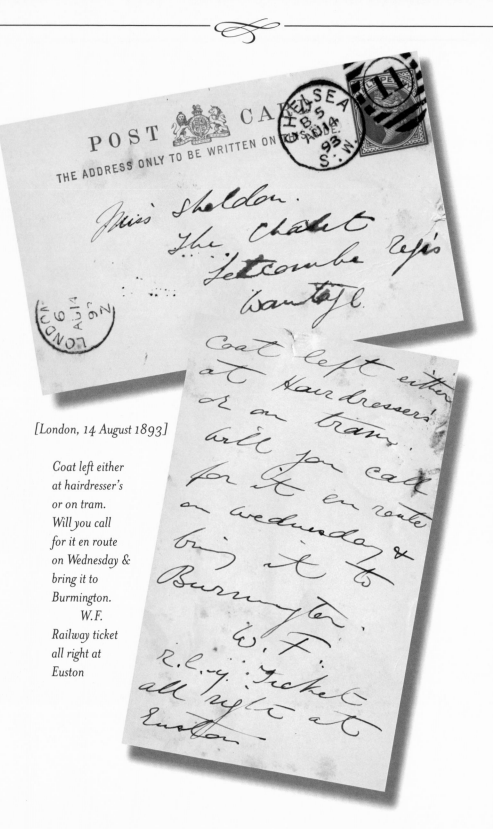

[London, 14 August 1893]

Coat left either
at hairdresser's
or on tram.
Will you call
for it en route
on Wednesday &
bring it to
Burmington.
    W.F.
Railway ticket
all right at
Euston

Watercolour by Percy French of the house adjacent to the Burmington mill, c. 1893. The mill is the building on the left, and Burmington House a short walk past the cottages.

The Mall
Baldoyle
[August 1893]

Darling Lennie

    I found on arriving in Dublin that Mecredy was off prospecting in Scotland for his cycle tour & Mrs M. & the others were to join him on Friday. This I heard from Miss Grimshaw who was installed in the editorial chair. I wrote to Mrs M. saying I would postpone my visit & then started for Baldoyle where I thought I would put in a week's hard sketching before tackling the west. I went out early & did a fairly good piece of work. I then had an impromptu bathe using a bit of a wreck as a springboard (no towel, as good Jaegerites never dry themselves) & after a light luncheon set off again. This time I found a very pleasant corner of a cornfield with the Dublin Mountains as a background, so I set to work & found my summer work beginning to tell for it really is the best thing I have done yet by a long way. This morning my movements have been again thrown into chaos by a letter from Mrs Mecredy saying that Mac. had left word that I was to come with them as their guest, good biz! dacent paple, so they are. It seems too good a chance to miss, but I shall stay a week here first, & put my affairs in order. They stay a fortnight away, but I shall only go for a week I think & drop the Godley expedition. I lunched with La Grimshaw & finding she could tell character by the face I showed her a small photo of you, & I think she made some good hits. This is what she said of my little sweetheart. She (Geliebtest) is living with someone she does not like – lives a repressed life, would like sometimes to say bitter things, but probably doesn't as she has a good deal of self control, has a great liking for pretty things, & has good artistic abilities preferring form to colour (portrait to landscape?) is affectionate & constant. Some sense of humour (snapshots?). Fond of travel, & musical. In fact just the wife for me! A cousin of mine has just turned up & seeing my last two pictures on the mantelpiece remarked 'Hullo! You are going in for oils' which shows the improvement in strength. How about the mill & house? I hope your father & mother are flourishing & that the former is able to distinguish the armorials in his birthday picture. Write soon beloved one to your longing-to-hold-you-once-more-in-my-arms Willie

Haven't time to get a P.O.O.[91] today.

Watercolour by Percy French of haystacks with the Dublin hills in the background.

Stewart's Mill Cottage
Brig O'Turk
Perthshire
[August 1893]

Darling of darlings,

The whirl we live in here makes it hard to find a minute to write a proper love letter, & the weather is so uncertain that when I see the sunshine I must run out & sketch. I am learning the language but received a rebuff from a native 'fushermon' who said he knew I was from Ireland. If you were only here life would be very perfect such heather clad mountains for you to run up & shady ravines to cuddle you in! The party consist of 3 gents and 6 ladies at present but two more men turn up on Monday. The life is a very free & easy one. The ladies march to the river about 8 oc. dressed in shoes & blankets & when they have had their swim the gents sally forth to what I call the 'ordeal by water' as it is very cold. 'The ordeal by sand' consists of rubbing yourself with the fine river sand which has a very warming & invigorating effect. The Mecredys supply the commissariat & have brought hams, plum puddings, tinned fruit &c to any amount for cyclists to eat. I part company with them after breakfast & set to work at the scenery, it is a little too green as yet but the strength of the mountain colours makes you use plenty of paint. Tea comes off about 7 & then we sing songs & choruses till 10. There is a project on foot to go & serenade the people in the Trossachs Hotel but I think our choir is rather too ragged (vocally) as yet. Mecredy has been away on business so I haven't had a talk with him yet however he seems anxious for my work so I daresay we will come to terms. I think your lion was very well drawn tho. she ended so abruptly. Send me a bit of a flower done in the open air with the tone of the natural background shown. I am always thinking of you & wanting you close close close to me so don't be afraid that I will stay away longer than I can help. Write very soon to your

more loving than ever

Willie

The steamship, *Rob Roy*.

LINES WRITTEN AFTER A BAD ATTACK O' "THE GAELIC"

Oh, Scotland is a bonnie lan',
The mountains grow on ev'ry han',
Ye'll ride frae Beersheba to Dan
   And mark them risin'.
And eh! The air is awfu' gran'
   An' appetisin'.

The windin' lakes that gem the scene,
The birken boughs and grasses green,
The birrin' patricks upward fleen,
   In sic a panic.
I note a' this an' mair between
   Twa bites o' bannock.

The shadows an' the shiftin' lights,
The dark ravines, the rocky heights,
The ants that choose their biggin sites
   In wondrous manner.
A' lifts yer soul in eagle flights
   (Man! When's ta dinner?).

'Tis fine to merk the torrent seethe,
Or clamber thro' the cloody wreath,
An' 'cooee' to the folk beneath
   In coach or carriage.
But don't forget to keep a breath
   To cool yer parritch.

Ye'd like to 'tow' a maid, perhaps? —
Weel, tak' advice frae knowin' chaps
An' to the highest mountain taps
  Ye'll easy lug her,
By takin' first a bowl o' 'saps'
  (Bread, milk, an' sugar).

An' noo I've sang o' oure delight,
An' if ye have na fo'lowed quite,
Still gather frae the words I write
  (An' dinna chortle),
A cyclist has an appetite
  That's mair than mortal.

An' if at my big meals ye stared
Ye should ha' seen hoo ithers fared,
Not fish, nor flesh, nor fowl was spared;
  Ye call me greedy,
I'm jest 'the fastin' mon' compared
  Wi' Dick Mecredy.

WILL WAGTALE

Brig O'Turk
[September 1893]

Darlingest

I am just in from a great day spent on the road between Loch Katrine **92** & Loch Lomond. The whole party started at 6.30 for Loch Katrine where we got on board the 'Rob Roy' & sailed down the lake 'thro the mists of morning' then cycled again to Loch Lomond (Inversnaid). The clan Mecredy then got on another steamer to Tarbet whence they intended cycling to Killin & then home by Callander as this meant an all day tour of 58 miles. I left them on the bonnie banks of Loch Lomond & wended my way slowly homewards. I had marked down several 'moory' bits on our morning ride so I spent the day securing them or perhaps I should say something entirely unlike them. Walking or leisurely cycling is the only way to see these places. The coaches hurry you thro. far too fast. I will be your guide, philosopher & best friend, sweetheart when we come here together. I leave this on Friday next for 'Ireland home & duty.' I have got a good idea of heath & rocks but the bracken has yet to be mastered. We went for a stroll up the river here (Glenfinglas) on Sunday & discovered 10 large anthills most of them about 2 feet high & made of fine needles & clay. The ants are about this size [pen drawing, 12mm]. I must look up the subject for no one seems to have heard of such large anthills before. I have seen 2 red deer a moor cock & a kingfisher in my wanderings, the caper calyie & the eagles still keep aloof.

So I compare favourably with other men do I – the same to you & many of them. There is only one girl in the world for me.

The others have turned up most of them apparently hale & hearty & calling for hot bread & milk which seems to be a satisfactory cyclist's supper. Scones & heather honey do for little me.

I enclose a tam o'shanter and not much gold

for my darling from her loving Willie

From a later letter to the family from R.J. Mecredy:

In 1889 the tour was to Scotland, and we camped near Brig o'Turk in Glen Finglass. When one member of the party, Tom Sealy, was due to return home, at an early hour my wife and I were aroused by a knock at the door. 'What's the matter?' I asked. 'I'm not sure,' said French, 'whether the stockings I'm wearing belong to RJ or the old Sealyham; if they belong to him I had better take them off.' On my inspecting them I found they were mine, so French was not deprived of his stockings.

One of the party was a Canon Whelan. On the evening of the day he arrived he was looking everywhere for his slippers, but in vain. He appealed to the party present. At this stage French began to take notice. 'Slippers,' he said, 'is it slippers? Better look at mine.' Sure enough, they belonged to Canon Whelan.

I have seen him with a boot belonging to one man and a shoe belonging to another, while his stockings were of different colours. A big army blanket which we used for camping concealed further deficiencies.

I shall never forget the appearance he presented solemnly parading the deck of the 'Rob Roy' on Loch Katrine, amidst a crowd of fashionably dressed tourists, with one of these army blankets draped round his stalwart figure, the broad arrow showing prominently in the middle of his back. They looked at him as though they thought he was an escaped convict.

Cloonyquin,⁹³ Tulsk
Co Roscommon
[September 1893]

Dearest darling

Here I am back in the old home at last & find a sweet little letter waiting for me.
I wish I had you here to show you all mine ancient haunts, however a time will come!
Well sweetheart we left the good old Brig O'Turk on Wednesday after a couple of successful
days up the Glen, most of us trained from Callender to Glasgow but the flying squad
scorned all assistance from steam & rode down to the boat. We there parted with Miss
Frost, a rather reserved English girl who however dissolved in tears on realizing that the
holiday among the wild Irishry was over so she must have enjoyed herself more than we
thought. We had a few hours in Glasgow so I did the art gallery & saw Whistler's great
picture of Carlisle, it reminds one of French's great picture of the Rev Shaw only less
refined. We (Miss Johnston experimental lecturer Alexandre College & Miss Davoresi of
Sydney Parade) saw a good many watercolours by David Cox & Peter de Wint but they
died before they were able to enjoy the privilege of coming out to sketch with me, so you
can fancy their work is not up to much. The two ladies I mention formed the most artistic
the least cycling & the worst sailing part of our society. We had a farewell concert on
board ship which seemed to please the passengers very much. The old programme 'Shine
shine moon', Swanee Ribber', 'Stable Jacket' &c. I ran out to Templeogue on returning to
interview the Dr but to no purpose as he only made his expenses in H. Show Week & lost
on the tour – just as well I didn't go with them. I called on McGuinness on my way back
& was told by him that my last Scotch sketches were all a great advance on anything I have
done yet, so also pronounced the only Orpen, so I am off to the bogs of Frenchpark ⁹⁴
tomorrow with high hopes. The Dean's wife here is anxious to get up a concert as a treat
for the congregation while I am here. She works it up & I take the proceeds which is
tempting. However Bogs & 'The Banshee' are the first consideration as time flies. Please
tell your mother she is doubtless right but I never could understand 'the proprieties.'
However I daresay she means well.⁹⁵ I stay here about 10 days & will go back to Dublin
via the Godleys I think. Mecredy expects me to stay with him but time will tell. & now
geliebtest shlaven si wole ⁹⁶ & dream of

your hopeful old lover

Willie

Watercolour by Percy French, 'On the Frenchpark Estate'.

Beloved Lennie

Just a line now to tell you to keep
up your spirits for you must be having
a very trying time. & I will write
again on Friday when the "Grand
Concert" will be over. Just now
I am trying to finish a couple of
pictures (orders) practise choruses
sketch from nature & work up some
songs & recitations of my own so n
mind is a little chaotic. I hope
Aunt Bell is improving in health
& spirits, & will soon be herself again.
The noble peasantry here think
I have "improved wonderful" but
oh Marther Willie didn't ye git
terrible grey". I think a ramble
with you about this old place
would be equal to the Downs
which is saying a good deal

Beloved Lennie

Just a line now to tell you to keep up your spirits for you must be having a very trying time, & I will write again on Friday when the "Grand Concert" will be over. Just now I am trying to push a couple of pictures (orders) practise choruses sketch from nature & work up some songs & recitations of my own so my mind is a little chaotic. I hope Aunt Bell is improving in health & spirits & will soon be herself again.

The noble peasantry here think I have "improved wonderful", 'but oh Masther Willie didn't ye get terrible grey!' I think a ramble with you about this old place would be equal to the Downs which is saying a good deal. Apropos what of Dorothy's picture? I have started Christine painting & she is very anxious to compare her work with yours. I hope the new domestic is a jewel – how do the lady helps get on at the Whittles? Hold yourself in readiness to be hugged in October by

your ever loving

Willie

Darlingest

    *I haven't very much to chronicle as one day is much the same as another here.
Breakfast at 9 after which Christopher Jnr & I have a game of tennis, then I go off to my
bog with some sandwiches & stay there till sunset; Christine is anxious to learn how to
paint so I have started her at tones & values. One of the small children here (Alice's
youngest) has been very ill, so my concert is postponed for a week, however the infant is
I think out of danger. A painter is a rare sight in Roscommon & the country people always
put me down as 'a government party makin' maps.' As usual people are most taken with
my bog pictures & I have got two orders already. I am going to call on the De Freynes
tomorrow (Saturday). He has been away voting against the Home Rule Bill (these
landowners are so prejudiced) & now that he feels safe may be inclined to squander his
gold on gems of art. Glad to hear Pauly has been keeping things lively, give him my best
thanks & ask him to teach you Poker as it might add to our income. How about Dorothy's
picture, is it time it was purchased by the unknown firm of millionaires? My Anne
Hathaway might go for what it will fetch as my work now is much better. I haven't started
my tour in the I.C. yet, as cycling & painting take up my time & brain. Send me an
autumn tint soon & tell me if you want paints. My father takes me to see striking views
here & then is surprised to find me sitting with my back to the view sketching a tree trunk
or some weeds, 'twas ever thus.*

    *Have not had time to finish so write from Frenchpark. A good day on the shores of
Lough Gara yesterday but raining hard today which is sad as besides heathers bogs have a
lot of red deer in the park which I wanted to have a shot at with a brush. I would like to
see your meadow sweet very much it would be an ornament to my foregrounds. I got your
letter just as I left Cloonyquin. I wonder who my Droitwich friends were? Did you ever
read Haweis's account of the Elijah in 'Music & Morals'* [97] *if not do so. There goes the
dinner bell. So goodbye my darling. There's a good time coming for both of us I think
soon so be hopeful.*

    Your loving

      Willie

Concert

Part I

Plantation Song and Chorus. 'Hear dem Bell[s]'

Comic Song — — — — — W P French

Sketch

'Our Local Penny Reading' W P French
Showing how we read and recite at these popular
(entertainment[s])

Plantation Song and Chorus. Swanee Ribber

Part II

Plantation Song and chorus. 'Tavern in Town'

Sketch

The Amateur Drama. Why I didn't become an Actor
W P French

Plantation Song & Chorus. Dancing Shoes

Part III

Plantation Song & Chorus. 'Traveling back to' Dixie
De ole Banjo

Sketch 'Snooping' or 'a brush with the natives'.
In this sketch Mr French will paint
a water colour sketch in 5 minutes

Plantation Song & Chorus — — — — — 'Good night.'

Cloonyquin
Tulsk
Friday
[September 1893]

Darlingest Lennie

The 'musical humourous & artistic entertainment' by W.P.F. is well over & I am about £12 to the good **98** over the transaction not a bad night's work – I had three sisters & the Dean's sister-in-law as chorus & our audience applauded every item. The stammering song, 'The Cats', & 'Mat Hannigan's Aunt' were the favourites & my inverted landscape took the fancy of the bucolic mind very much. One large farmer informed us afterwards it was a most 'classical entertainment.' You mightn't think this judging from the programme. We had the Huzzarenritt as an overture (played by the Misses French) on a very tinny piano. They hadn't practised it, so the Huzzars proceeded with considerable caution. We wanted your nimble fingers Dearie. The 'quality' of Roscommon want me to give a concert in the capital town, which is rather tempting as they give you the Grand Jury room (holding 400) for nothing. However we shall see. Let me know when I may appear at mine ancient haunts.

The weather here is very broken & I am not doing all I wanted in the sketching line. However today I had a stroke of luck & put in the sky & middle distance of my largest & most important work! It happened thus. I had stretched a full sized sheet of drawing paper on the frame of an old window sash, so that I could use both sides of the paper. The back I used last night for my lightning water colour 'Le retoor from le marchet' but the front was still unprofaned by hand of man. This morning I happened to see some glorious clouds rolling by my cock loft so I hastily damped the already painted side of my paper & proceeded to dash in a bold French cum Constable sky on the other. The result is very happy & a moor done from some studies looks very fine in the middle distance. I am going over to Frenchpark again tomorrow to get a good foreground & then let the Dublin sketching club 'clear the line.' Today I want £12 down for it, but there will probably be a reaction tomorrow & I shall say in the words of La tante Harrigan 'Pourquoi etes vous tete montée?' **99** I see our little Doctor is advertising 'a few more seats to be had' which is Collissonese for 'lots of room yet.' I am really going for him after his first concert on the 6th Oct. I am enclosing £1 from the committee of the Chantry Bequest for the purchase of 'Anne Hathaway's Cottage' (D. Baird) if you can get it for 15/- the chairman suggests that you keep the change. And now dearest Lennie I must be off to my little cat so goodbye sweetheart & take special care of yourself for the sake of your loving

Willie

I hope Aunt Bell is getting better, send me the latest bulletin.

Watercolour by Percy French of Cloonyquin, painted the following year.
Ettie is in the pram being pushed by Lennie, beyond the tree.

Darling

A hurried line to say I forgot to enclose £1 in my last as you may have noticed. A note from Alfred Godley this morning to say he is engaged to a Miss Cay – 'a saxon, but after all there must be Saxons.' He is at his Leitrim home **100** & wants me to call in on my way to Dublin. I may do so as the vicinity is <u>boggy</u>, & I haven't half enough pictures for the sketching club yet. I am off on a bicycle to church so fare thee well my own true love, fare thee well for a while.

Your loving

Willie

Just got yours – Dearest I can't get over to you yet as the rain here has kept me from doing much & I will want a few days at Baldoyle to make pictures of my studies. I have just been looking at my Burmington sketch book & am surprised at my progress since I came over here. That is bad news about Woolford Fields. Can I do anything? I want an evening with you immensely – but I think if I can make a big splash with the bogs at the Sketching Club this month it will bring the time nearer when we can be always together. Think of that Sweetheart!!! My big picture still looks well which is hopeful.

Your working &

loving Willie

Drominchin,
Carrigallen,
Co Leitrim
[September 1893]

Best beloved

I don't at all like disappointing you – and myself, & this putting of business before pleasure is rather unusual with me, still I see in my calmer moments that this invitation to the Godleys is a great chance & must be made the most of. I am surrounded by mountain & moor in fact I haven't to go past the avenue gate to get a view of purple mountains & brown bog. I sent seven pictures to Belfast. The Exh. opened on Monday last & I had a postcard on Thursday to say a bog was sold (£2.10)! Alfred Godley has departed to his 'dona's' residence, **101** *Hazlemere, to be inspected by her relatives. He 'hopes he is conducting himself with propriety but fears they miss that look of profundity one expects in a College Don.' Mrs Godley's soldier son brought home a wife of an advanced Simla type & she was not a success, so Mrs G is a little anxious about her excellent eldest born. One of the labourers here is a poet & wants to start as a writer professionally. I was called in as an expert but could not encourage him as the very best poetry (my own) only brought in £1 a week. The butler has a fiddle (he made himself!) which I am to interview tomorrow, so you perceive what a talented race the Irish are. I saw Miss June Shaw's ride of 212 miles in 24 hours mentioned in last P. M. Gazette. I hope your mother was edified thereat.*

A great day in the bog, just finished 2 good pictures & some valuable figures of men at work. The most usual attitude when at work is both arms on top of spade pipe in mouth & hat over eyes. Christine says you had the advantage of her in beginning to paint before she did so you must send over a specimen first. She is at present rather proud of a 'landscape with wheelbarrow', but it is not equal in merit to your justly celebrated 'study of leaves'. Maud Godley works in oils a little so I have been showing her what an optical feast a bog hole is. The family hope to make your acquaintance at an early date, there's a good time coming sweetheart. Just got yours, I don't think I ought to leave this till the 28th and even on wet days I make studies of cabin interiors with their quaint inhabitants, good for future illustrations & C. Mascheroni says he has enough to do in Act I to last him till his return. Another small cheque from Gobbins, so 'que voulez vous encore' dit la tante Hannigan. I would that I were 'wandering' round Burmington but the seas divide us. I am always your

loving Willie

Vallumbrosa
Nr Bray
Co Dublin
[October 1893]

Beloved & Best

    I leave this for Burmington on Thursday morning or evening, so get ready your best hug. Great projects on here. Mecredy wants me to go into a tremendous cycling paper which starts in London in December & is to swallow up all others. He edits from Dublin & has sub. ed. in London & will take prose, verse & illustrations from me. We had a meeting of the new staff here (the old set & 3 London men) & they seem very confident & have any amount of money to back it up. I went up to see how they had hung my pictures yesterday & also to write an article for the Social Review & had quite an ovation from the artists on the strength of my work (all hung but 3). People writing already to know if I would teach a class. I was looking at my Burmington sketches to-day & they are very weak. I was also congratulated by M. Christien on my Belfast exhibit. So my prices are going up, better apply for shares very soon. The Social Review seems anxious to make me a permanence but they don't pay very much yet,

    yr loving

    Willie

Watercolour by Percy French.

61 Carlisle Mansions
Victoria Str
[October? 1893]

Dearest Lennie,

Better say Monday 16th for our tour. I haven't done as much as I could wish as
yet as I have had to make appointments to meet my editorial friends. Dowdswell seemed to
like my colouring but said I must bring some finished pictures for him to look at before he
could promise an exhibit. Braxton Smith (of our Irish tour) took me down to Sunbury
from Sat. to Monday, where we lay around in a heat in a backwater & lazed. I have to
renounce Paris & all its works as I think it is better to stay here at Braxton's & look up
friends. Let me know the hour you will be at Reading. Glad to hear you are sketching.
Don't try the sky out of doors & send me anything you do. Consider yourself hugged

by your loving

Willie

Dearest Beloved

Most kissable & distinctly hugsome. I was very glad to get your little note & to find that we both felt our parting was hurried & unsatisfactory. We both thought it all wrong which makes it all right. Rather an Irish way of putting it but we know what we mean.

Well I got 3/4 of an hour at the pictures in Birmingham & saw enough to show me I am on the right track in trying to paint light and shade effects. I saw Skiddy's large picture of sheep hung a trifle high but looking well. The clouds not quite maddled enough I think. I found the storm had subsided at Holyhead & we had a fine passage leaving me quite up to concert pitch. I fixed on a very fine room for my studio, 12 Dawson Str, [102] but haven't come to terms with the landlord yet. You will find a short poem by Orpen in last week's review. My story is in next number which I will forward tomorrow.

Mullingar took to me kindly last night & I am giving a show tonight at the Mullingar lunatic asylum. They say I will be quite 'en rapport' with my audience.

I find I can't play the intermezzo yet. A Miss O'Donnell (pupil of Joachim [103]) played it last night magnificently, another girl (a rival) also played — 'but oh the difference to me.' Mecredy telegraphs for 'copy' so must start at once.

Ever your loving

lover Willie

Aboard the good ship *Munster*
Sunday. 8 bells.
wind astern,
t'gan sels & royals set.
all taut (except the writer
who is untaught)

Beloved & best

You will see from the above
that I am on the high seas. and
speeding for London, fame & fortune,
M. Christie has been lecturing on
art & mentioned W.P.F. as a coming
star in the landscape world. I havn't
come to terms with the landlord of
12 Dawson Street yet. as he wants
me to take another room as well as
the studio, but I have a scheme on
hand which may suit all parties. Orpen
is going to set up an office for himself
so I have just written to him to go
& look at the other room, if he
took it, it would be very pleasant
to have such a congenial neighbour.
I have 7 pupils

The paddle steamer *S.S. Munster* leaving
Kingstown (now Dun Laoghaire).

Aboard the good ship Munster
Sunday. 8 bells.
Wind astern.
t'gansels & royals set.
all taut (except the writer
who is untaught)
[November? 1893]

Beloved & best

You will see from the above that I am on the high seas and speeding for London, fame & fortune. M. Christien has been lecturing on art & mentioned W.P.F. as a coming star in the landscape world. I haven't come to terms with the landlord of 12 Dawson Street yet, as he wants me to take another room as well as the studio, but I have a scheme on hand which may 'suit all parties'. Orpen is going to set up an office for himself so I have just written to him to go & look at the other room, if he took it, it would be very pleasant to have such a congenial neighbour.

I have 7 pupils promised already
[2 pages missing, most likely withheld by Ettie]
see pages 2 & 3

by Bismarch. (spelling no defect)

Gretchen gretchen 104
Gib mir dein antwort, da
Ich bin auger mich, von liebe — ja
Für den Heimraths' tag — s'ist schaden!
Komm nicht in wagen haben
Ach Donner und Blitz
So schon sie sitz
Auf ein Neiderad g'mackt für zwei!

If George Moore has criticised the New English art club in the Speaker you might send it to me, as I am going there this week — and now beloved I must away — I finish this at Euston — things are going well — there's to be a wedding at the end of January & don't you forget it. Pas une mariage de hauteur but the after life will be very sweet to
your loving
Willie

Charles Manners & Fanny Moody, 'A Bicycle Built for Two'.

Irish Society 1894

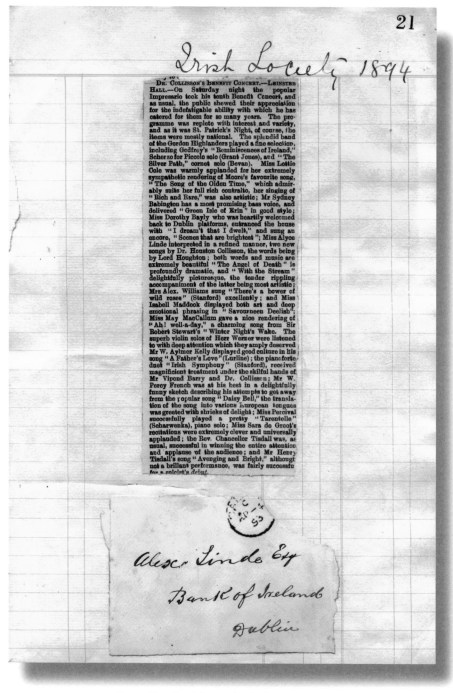

Dr. Collisson's Benefit Concert.—Leinster Hall.—On Saturday night the popular Impresario took his tenth Benefit Concert, and as usual, the public shewed their appreciation for the indefatigable ability with which he has catered for them for so many years. The programme was replete with interest and variety, and as it was St. Patrick's Night, of course, the items were mostly national. The splendid band of the Gordon Highlanders played a fine selection, including Godfrey's "Reminiscences of Ireland," Scherzo for Piccolo solo (Grant Jones), and "The Silver Path," cornet solo (Bevan). Miss Lottie Cole was warmly applauded for her extremely sympathetic rendering of Moore's favourite song, "The Song of the Olden Time," which admirably suits her full rich contralto, her singing of "Rich and Rare," was also artistic; Mr Sydney Babington has a most promising bass voice, and delivered "Green Isle of Erin" in good style; Miss Dorothy Bayly who was heartily welcomed back to Dublin platforms, entranced the house with "I dream't that I dwelt," and sung an encore, "Scenes that are brightest"; Miss Alyce Linde interpreted in a refined manner, two new songs by Dr. Houston Collisson, the words being by Lord Houghton; both words and music are extremely beautiful "The Angel of Death" is profoundly dramatic, and "With the Stream" delightfully picturesque, the tender rippling accompaniment of the latter being most artistic; Mrs Alex. Williams sung "There's a bower of wild roses" (Stanford) excellently; and Miss Isabell Maddock displayed both art and deep emotional phrasing in "Savourneen Deelish"; Miss May MacCallum gave a nice rendering of "Ah! well-a-day," a charming song from Sir Robert Stewart's "Winter Night's Wake. The superb violin solos of Herr Werner were listened to with deep attention which they amply deserved Mr W. Aylmer Kelly displayed good culture in his song "A Father's Love" (Lurline); the pianoforte duet "Irish Symphony" (Stanford), received magnificent treatment under the skilful hands of Mr Vipond Barry and Dr. Collisson; Mr W. Percy French was at his best in a delightfully funny sketch describing his attempts to get away from the popular song "Daisy Bell," the translation of the song into various European tongues was greeted with shrieks of delight; Miss Percival successfully played a pretty "Tarentelle" (Scharwenka), piano solo; Miss Sara de Groot's recitations were extremely clever and universally applauded; the Rev. Chancellor Tisdall was, as usual, successful in winning the entire attention and applause of the audience; and Mr Henry Tisdall's song "Avenging and Bright," although not a brilliant performance, was fairly successful for a soloist's *debut.*

Alex. Linde Esq

Bank of Ireland

Dublin

From Alyce Lindé's scrapbooks from 1894.[105]

Braemuir House
Norwood
[December 1893]

Dearest & Best

The 26th is an excellent date. Earlier if you like. It is a beautiful time that is coming and cannot come too soon for me. I'm only afraid you will be giving yourself no rest in order to have everything ready. I haven't done or seen much here as we live at Norwood & I have to put in an appearance at the Crystal Palace **106** every day, so I only did a few morning performances in London. I saw Corney Grain & was surprised to hear him sing the chorus of 'Dysy' in French. He is supposed to be a good linguist but our version is much the best. He uses our discarded 'chic & pic' & talks of 'un bicycle fait pour deux' which is not idiomatic enough for my fastidious ear. I went to several picture galleries & was able to detect a lot of landscape work done in the studio so my knowledge of nature is increasing evidently. I must get into these galleries soon, for the prices they ask & frequently get are enormous. I have interviewed Brindley about a cottage ornée but have come to no conclusion yet. If I find myself getting flurried I shall take lodgings for a while & then we can look round & furnish at our leisure.* I got offers for a good many of my pictures but didn't take them as they will do for coming exhibitions, so I only made £9 off the sketching club, however I get any amount of praise for my work which will help towards a class.

*A lot of our time will be spent in the studio where you will I think have a reception room of your own, fitted up in a style worthy of the Queen of my heart. Jot down any ideas for the Cycle which come into your reliable little head. I am working up your Mormon idea for the Xmas number. Christine is a very shy young person & would be quite at sea among new faces, however the family are all ready to receive & love you when you arrive. This is a very disjointed letter as there are cyclists fibbering round. Look out for me on Saturday before Xmas eve.

Your loving

Willie

The paper & printing of 'the Cycle' will be improved on shortly.

The Mall
Baldoyle
[December 1893]

Dearest & Sweetest

*All goes well. I have secured the Studio & am busy (very) fitting it up.
The Dean of Magdalen will be best man, he writes to say he will be glad to assist as his
own affair comes off at Easter & he wants to see how the thing works as otherwise he
'might get christened or ordained.' I gave a very successful lecture at Carlow, the audience
picking up every point. The Social Review wrote to me for 12 lines of verse (sentimental)
describing a picture of a girl sitting under a tree & thinking evidently (with a pleased
expression) of her lover. There is not much in the result — which I wrote on the steamer,
except alliteration. Just had a note from Manners asking if I had any bogs on hand as
he wants a couple 'good biz.' I think if the class is in full swing in Jan. we had better
spend the honeymoon among the sandhills & seagulls of Baldoyle as I must be on or
about the studio.*

*A begging letter from Mecredy just came in to know where that Xmas story is,
so I must tackle it before post. Orpen is not leaving Drew's office yet but a nice young
fellow named Brooks also an assistant of Drew's is leaving next week & takes my third
room at No 12, Dawson Str. I got some fine tips on banjo playing in London & play
airs in harmonies now!*

*Are you getting up a concert, if so let it be in Xmas week as I must get back as soon
after New Year's Day as possible. Can I get to Burmington on Sunday? You might look
up trains for me. Collisson talks of tours but 'I am off — dead off.' I must dart into town
now sweetheart so goodbye till next week. I am always thinking of you & looking forward
to the times when no letters will be necessary.*

Ever your

loving Willie

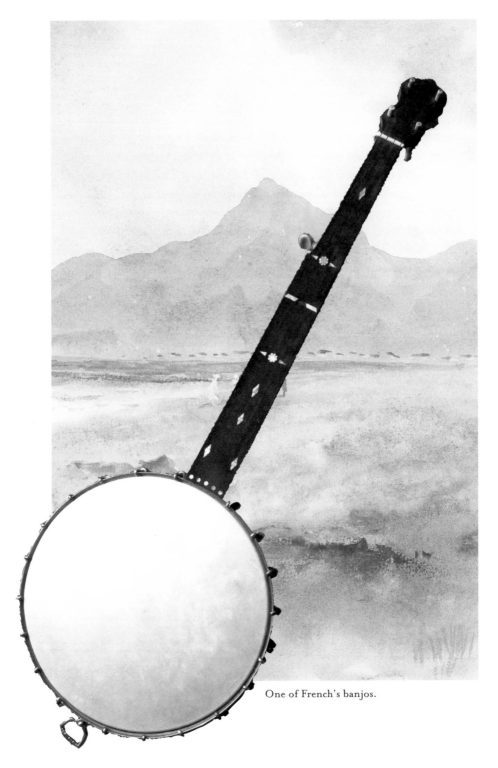

One of French's banjos.

The Mall
Baldoyle
[January 1894]

Beloved & best

 I have lots to tell you but can't find a minute. Only 3 out of my 7 promises have turned up yet which is bad, but the dauntless three find they learn a lot & are telling friends to come which is good. McGuinness tells me he never gets people to come till end of Jan. so all may yet be well, meanwhile I am 'laying very low.' I sent off two pictures to Oldham Exch, (where I have friends) & am sending next week to Leeds. I saw pictures in Manchester, Birmingham & Liverpool & am beginning to think highly of my own. Am writing a Scotch guide for Mecredy & getting studio ready for you. I intend having Mrs. P.O'D. to tea there next week & some other good gossips which should bear fruit. I want you very much & don't seem able to settle down till I have you curled up in the old armchair. Tell your father the insurance is being settled up all right.

 Ever your

  lover

   Willie

[January 1894]

Best & most beloved

    I have so much to think of that I know not if head or heels are uppermost. My class has increased to 6 which experts say is very promising for a start, two days a week from 10 to 2. I have to get some good pictures ready for the R.H.A. before I leave as I don't suppose much will be done on our Lune de Nuit! I haven't found a house yet. The Howth people like letting their houses for the summer at high rents, so we may have to come nearer town. Your presents seem to be very fine & ornamental. Mine as yet are the practical, chiefly articles for the studio, a carpet, a coal scuttle & a wash hand stand. I have all the usual things already. Mrs Hanley is busy fitting up the Mall for your reception, but I tell her to make no permanent improvements as we are birds of passage.

    The studio you will like I think tho. it's not all my fancy painted it. The painter says (like Sullivan's workman) that 'it will come right after a bit.' I'm afraid I won't get away before Monday evg. So will miss the village tea. I want you over here dearie to look after me. Only a week today & I shall have you for good & all! Hurrah! The ring is bought, & the certificate ready. Must be off to prepare for class.

    Your about to be

        husband

          Willie

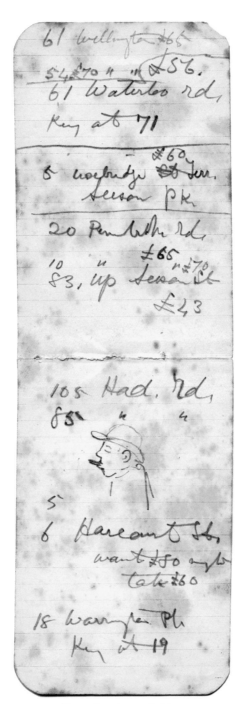

House hunting in Dublin.

12 Dawson Str
Friday night
Jan 19 [1894]

Darlingest

    Just a line to wish you joy. I am feathering the nest to the best of my ability, but my coffers are not overflowing, however the Class is catching on & I have 7 now, & they seem struck with the ability of their teacher. **107** *I give a farewell lesson on Monday, & set them a holiday task.*

    I wired the number of the insurance policy & the date to Burmington today as your mother said Alfred H. would be there. He & you had better fix up the settlements, I am too busy with the present to feign even a polite interest in posthumous affairs. I find the draft is out at Baldoyle. I go there Sunday & will forward it. My elder brother Arthur St George French will act as trustee if required.

    I am in a fuss just now but am & will be always

       Your lover

         Willie

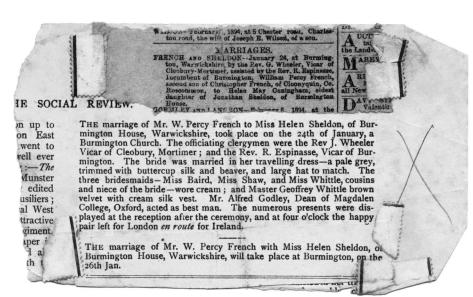

IE SOCIAL REVIEW.

on up to
on East
went to
vell ever
:—The
Munster
edited
usiliers;
al West
ttractive
giment.
per
l a
th

THE marriage of Mr. W. Percy French to Miss Helen Sheldon, of Burmington House, Warwickshire, took place on the 24th of January, a Burmington Church. The officiating clergymen were the Rev J. Wheeler Vicar of Cleobury, Mortimer; and the Rev. R. Espinasse, Vicar of Burmington. The bride was married in her travelling dress—a pale grey, trimmed with buttercup silk and beaver, and large hat to match. The three bridesmaids—Miss Baird, Miss Shaw, and Miss Whittle, cousins and niece of the bride—wore cream; and Master Geoffrey Whittle brown velvet with cream silk vest. Mr. Alfred Godley, Dean of Magdalen College, Oxford, acted as best man. The numerous presents were displayed at the reception after the ceremony, and at four o'clock the happy pair left for London *en route* for Ireland.

THE marriage of Mr. W. Percy French with Miss Helen Sheldon, of Burmington House, Warwickshire, will take place at Burmington, on the 26th Jan.

From the French family scrapbooks.[108]

The church of St Barnabas and St Nicholas, Burmington.

The marriage was on 24 January 1894 in the parish church at Burmington. The marriage certificate shows William Percy French, 39, Widower, Artist, of Baldoyle, Howth, Co. Dublin, father Christopher French, Gentleman, marrying Helen May Cunningham Sheldon, 25, Spinster, of Burmington, father Jonathan Sheldon, Miller. Witnesses are Dorothy Charlotte Baird, Alfred Denis Godley, J. Sheldon, L. Shaw and B.C.E. Tribe.

Lennie and Willie now married and in their first home, the studio at 12 Dawson Street, Dublin, she aged twenty-six and he thirty-nine. Rex is at their feet.

Afterword

Watercolour by Percy French of the canal at Mespil Road, Dublin.

Though their first home together was the studio in Dawson Street, Dublin, before long the couple acquired a house at 35 Mespil Road, Dublin. French sent postcards to their friends: 'We are living by the canal: do drop in'.

On 5 November of that year the first of three daughters was born, Ettie Gwendoline, named after French's first wife Ethel. French sent a postcard announcing the birth: 'A small French lady came last night (10.30) find it very hard to make her understand our language. All well. W.P.F.'

On 13 March 1896 Mollie Helen was born. In the winter of 1899/1900, with French finally deciding to seek his fame and fortune in London, he moved with the family to 21 Clifton Hill, St John's Wood.[109]

Studio photograph of Lennie, Mollie and Ettie in London.

On 26 April 1903 a third daughter, Joan Phyllis, was born.

By now French was earning his living as an entertainer, usually on his own but sometimes with a partner, and later with a small company. He continued painting watercolours, and was at his happiest while doing this.

In January 1905 they moved to 48 Springfield Road, in the same neighbourhood.

On 10 January 1908 Lennie's stepmother died and was buried at Burmington on 14 January.

Mollie, Ettie, Lennie and Joan.

In July 1910 the French family moved back to Clifton Hill, to No. 27.

Lennie had this photograph taken of herself and their three daughters and sent to her husband while he was on tour in the USA in 1910. He wrote to them: 'My dear friends, the gallery of fair females arrived on Christmas Day, so, in the words of Francis Farrelly, "I could hang them up to look at them and not feel so forlorn".'

This man of jests & man of jibes
as Doctor we accost
One of the celebrated Tribes
unhappily not 'Lost'.

The only existing drawing of any of Lennie's family apart from her is this one
of Dr Tribe, her cousin.[110]

In January 1919 their silver wedding was celebrated, when French penned these lines for Lennie:

> If we had lived upon our lone
> And never married - golly
> By now an ancient cat I'd own
> And you a pretty Polly.
> But such a course I think we've shown
> Had been surpassing folly
> For where would Ettie be! and Joan!
> And need I mention Mollie!

French, banjo in hand, with Lennie on an Irish side-car.

On 9 March 1919 Lennie's father Jonathan died and was buried at Burmington on the thirteenth.[111]

On 24 January 1920 French died, aged sixty-five,[112] after performing at an engagement in Glasgow. He was buried at Formby, Lancashire, where he had been staying at the time with his cousin, Canon Richardson. The family remained in London until in 1948 Lennie and her daughter Ettie moved to Monks Eleigh in Suffolk, Mollie and Joan taking a flat in London.

None of the daughters had married, their coming of age coinciding with the Great War. Ettie described her mother in these words: 'musical, an unusually good pianist, very human, profoundly interested in other people, and thoroughly convinced that life was worth living'.

Mollie died on 2 June 1956 aged sixty, and not long afterwards Lennie died, on 2 September, at the age of eighty-eight. A nephew has written:

> She was to me a wonderful person in many ways. I never had a talk with her without feeling stimulated by her intellectual alertness. She was also one of the few who could listen as well as talk. Her strong and unbiased sense of "family" always appealed to me.

Ettie died on 15 June 1993, in her ninety-ninth year, and Joan on 24 June 1996, in her ninety-fourth, both still living up to their death in the sixteenth century house in Monks Eleigh. Lennie is buried at St Peter's Church, Monks Eleigh, and her three daughters share the same grave.

'My white haired Laddie', painted by Lennie.

Notes

1   Ethel is buried in Mount Jerome Cemetery, Dublin, and the baby in the grounds of the now demolished Elphin Cathedral, Co. Roscommon, not far from Cloonyquin.

2   Lennie's birth certificate names Helen May Cunningham Sheldon, born Burmington 31 July 1868, father Jonathan Sheldon, Miller, mother Mary Clementina Sheldon, formerly Tribe, from the Liberty of Kidbrooke, in Lewisham. Mary's father, Thomas Tribe, was Secretary of the Belvedere Institution.

3   Ettie French's delightfully informative book *Willie* is published by the Percy French Society, Holywood 1994. The quotations in my *Afterword* are taken from this book. Ettie also mentions that an ancestor of Lennie was Lord Mayor of Dublin at the same time, 1691, as an ancestor of Willie was Mayor of Galway.

4   Rosabel, *née* Charter, Lennie's stepmother, was born c. 1845 and married Jonathan in Llanaber, Merionethshire, in 1874. She was a daughter of the surgeon John Charter. Jonathan's father, Thomas Izod Sheldon, described on the marriage certificate as 'Retired Farmer', attended. Rosabel died on 10 January 1908 aged sixty-four. During the period between wives, the family home included a housekeeper, nursemaid, and two servants domestic (1871 census). By 1881 there was a governess.

5   Ethel Grace Sheldon, born 24 October 1869, when aged eighteen married Robert Whittle, twenty-six, bachelor farmer from Wolford, which is very close to Burmington, in Burmington Parish Church on 27 March 1888.

6   French writes from 70 Redesdale Street, Chelsea, a lodging house run by Mary Harper. The street is near the old Chelsea Town Hall, and the artistic community lived in the area.

7   *Strongbow* was performed in Dublin at the Queen's Royal Theatre, Great Brunswick Street, built in 1844 and demolished in 1969. The theatre became the first home of the Abbey Theatre in 1904. The street is now named Pearse Street, and Pearse House stands on the site. The original production of *Strongbow* was never repeated. The first invasion was in 1169, so this was 'the second invasion'.

8   Dr W.A. Houston Collisson was the Dublin organist, conductor and impresario who accompanied French in his shows and wrote music for some sixteen of his songs, as well as the musical shows. He was a high-churchman, ordained in 1898. His autobiography, *Dr Collisson in and on Ireland*, gives a good account of his musical tours. He died on 1 February 1920, a week after conducting a funeral service for his great friend Percy French.

9   There was a Gaiety Theatre on Aldwych, London, but French is referring to the Gaiety Theatre in Dublin, opened in 1871. His reference to parting at Stafford shows that they were on their way back from Dublin via Holyhead and thence by train. He went on to London and she to Burmington.

10   'A propos des bottes' (French) means changing the subject.

11   Photograph of French by William R. Kennan, 41 Grafton Street, Dublin.

12   *Les Cloches de Corneville* is a comic opera by Robert Planquette, first performed in 1877. It became one of the most popular operettas of all time, with hit productions in London and elsewhere.

13   The two nights that Lennie 'came to see Strongbow' were most likely her being allowed time off to see the production from the auditorium.

14   James Henry Mapleson, 1830-1901, was the English opera impresario, at one time the leading light in London in that field. He had been manager of the Theatre Royal, Drury Lane, and he also started building a National Opera House on the Embankment, never completed. By 1892 he was bankrupt.

15   The houses in Redesdale Street were renumbered after a bomb fell on the east end of the street in WW2. After looking at old maps and census returns I believe that No. 70 is now No. 12.

16   Jonathan 'Jon' Sheldon was born 14 August 1841 at Burmington. He was the miller, employing fifteen men at the time of the 1881 census. His father Thomas (c. 1804-1878) was the miller before him and Thomas's wife was Elizabeth, *née* Hurlston (c. 1807-1884). Jonathan's brother Henry died aged four, his other brother Arthur aged ten months and his sister Catherine aged fifteen years. Thomas is in the 1851 census described as 'Milller, Baker & Farmer', employing fifteen men. In 1861 he is employing ten men and four boys with ninety-eight acres.

17   Moreton was the rail connection for Shipston. When the Oxford, Worcester and Wolverhampton Railway opened there in 1851 the line was known locally as the 'Old Worse and Worse Line'.

18   Mrs Gamp, an alcoholic midwife specializing in mangling speech, is a character in Charles Dickens' *Martin Chuzzlewit*.

19   Jonathan Sheldon, miller, was twelve years French's senior, and his wife Rosabel ten years French's senior.

20   The west wing of Burmington House, on the left in the photo, is a later addition. Lennie lived first in the Mill House, but by the time she met French was living in Burmington House. The house was built in 1828.

21 Corney Grain, 1844-1895, was a lawyer who gave it all up to become an entertainer and songwriter, writing social sketches and songs with piano. He clearly influenced French.

22 'Venice' was recreated at Olympia in London in 1892, comprising gondola trips on canals and showing scenes from Venetian life, with a cast of 1400 including a corps de ballet of 400.

23 This lovely sketch of Lennie was made by the Irish artist Walter Osborne (1859-1903) at one of the sketching classes. After study in Antwerp he moved to Brittany, then to England, and only returned to Ireland in 1892. He died at the age of forty-three from pneumonia, on the brink of artistic maturity.

24 *Soldiers Three* has words and music by Percy French.

25 *The Starving Man* has apparently not survived.

26 Richard D'Oyly Carte, 1844-1901, was the theatrical impresario and hotelier. He built two theatres and the Savoy Hotel, and brought together Gilbert and Sullivan.

27 *The Times of London* review of the production at St James' Theatre commented 'In point of polish its interpretation leaves nothing to be desired.' Oscar Wilde, 1854-1900, was born in the same year as French, and it was in the early 1890s that he became one of London's most popular playwrights.

28 The two decorated envelopes measure 96mm x 122mm. The letters measure 178 x 113mm before folding.

29 French walked from Burmington to Stratford, a distance of about twelve miles.

30 The Lyric Theatre on London's Shaftesbury Avenue was built in 1888 and is still there in 2015, the oldest theatre on the avenue. In its early days it staged mostly comic operas.

31 Alfred D. Godley, 1856-1925, was the son of the Rev. James Godley, Rector of Carigallen, Co. Leitrim. Godley had been a childhood friend of French, between them writing the comic magazines *Tulsk Morning Howl* and *The Trombone of Truth*. He became Public Orator at Oxford and Dean of Magdalen College. He wrote several collections of poetry.

32 *A Pantomime Rehearsal* was the play by Cecil Clay, from 1891.

33 The parish church at Stoke Newington in north London was designed by William Butterfield and completed in 1853.

34 The Great Western Hotel, now the Hilton London Paddington, is at Praed Street, Paddington. It opened in 1854 under the management of Isambard Kingdom Brunel himself. It is designed in the style of Louis XIV and is in effect the front of the station.

35   Lennie's birthday was 31 July.

36   This photograph of Houston Collisson is by the London society photographer E.H. Mills, who also took photos for French.

37   Horace Sedger was manager of the Lyric Theatre, Hammersmith.

38   'Dr C' refers to Dr Houston Collisson, who wrote the music for *Love All*.

39   Frederic Farrar was a cleric, author and schoolteacher. By all accounts he was an eloquent preacher and voluminous author.

40   On the second envelope French adds as an afterthought 'Burmington', missing in the previous envelope. Note his spelling, 'Warickshire', on both envelopes! And note that he does not need to specify which Miss Sheldon, as Lennie's younger sister is already away from home.

41   The Bairds, living at the Chalet, Letcombe Regis, Wantage, were relatives of Lennie. 'Aunt Grace', sister of Lennie's mother, was at the time a Lady's Companion to the head of the house, Jessie Silver. Grace's daughter was Dorothy. Lennie is staying there at the time of this letter.

42   Francis Day & Hunter were music publishers.

43   The Henley Regatta is a rowing event held since 1839 at Henley-on-Thames.

44   8/0 = 8 shillings, 0 pence, in the old LSD system of pounds, shillings and pence. 8 shillings is equivalent to forty pence in the metric pound. Average annual earnings in Britain in 1892 were £60.

45   Charles Whitmore stood as a Conservative in the UK general election of 1892 which took place on 26 July. The Conservatives won the greatest number of seats, but not enough for an overall majority. Gladstone formed a minority government which was dependent on the Irish Nationalists for support.

46   Hans Richter was the Hungarian conductor, prominent at Wagner's theatre in Bayreuth, and who worked regularly in England. He became a great supporter of Elgar's music: the *Second Symphony* is dedicated to him, and he is portrayed in the fourth movement.

47   'Pony' Moore and Frederic Burgess were surviving members of the *English Christy Minstrels*, a 'blackface group'. The troupe was renamed the *Moore & Burgess Minstrels*, numbering about thirty performers. They performed at St James' Hall, Piccadilly, for thirty-five years.

48   *The Pall Mall Gazette* was an evening newspaper founded in 1865.

49 'The Motor Bus' by Alfred Godley, with 'translation' and cases:

What is this that roareth thus?	What is this that roareth thus?
Can it be a Motor Bus?	Can it be a Motor Bus?
	(singular nominative case)
Yes, the smell and hideous hum	Yes, the smell and hideous hum
Indicat Motorem Bum!	Indicates a Motor Bus!
	(singular accusative case)
Implet in the Corn and High	Active in the Corn and High
	(colloquial names of streets)
Terror me Motoris Bi:	Terror of the Motor Bus:
	(singular genitive case)
Bo Motori clamitabo	I will shout out to the Motor Bus
	(singular dative case)
Ne Motore caedar a Bo---	Lest I am killed by the Motor Bus-
	(singular ablative case)
Dative be or Ablative	Dative be or Ablative
So thou only let us live:---	So thou only let us live:-
Whither shall thy victims flee?	Whither shall thy victims flee?
Spare us, spare us, Motor Be!	Spare us, spare us, O Motor Bus!
	(singular vocative case)
Thus I sang; and still anigh	Thus I sang, and still anigh
Came in hordes Motores Bi,	Came in hordes of Motor Buses,
	(plural genitive case)
Et complebat omne forum	And loads of Motor Buses
	(plural nominative case)
Copia Motorum Borum.	Filled up the whole forum.
	(plural nominative case)
How shall wretches live like us	How shall wretches live like us
Cincti Bis Motoribus?	Surrounded by Motor Buses?
	(plural ablative case)
Domine, defende nos	O Lord, defend us
Contra hos Motores Bos!	Against these Motor Buses!
	(plural accusative case)

50 The Dublin Horse Show, formed in 1864, has since been a showpiece for Ireland's equestrian talent. It takes place in July and is a great social event.

51 The Bairds were close relatives of Lennie. One was later a bridesmaid at the wedding.

52 Sir Herbert Beerbohm Tree, 1853-1917, was the English actor and theatre manager. This critically acclaimed production of *Hamlet* at the Haymarket Theatre in 1892 established Tree as a Shakespearean leading man.

53   *Lorna Doone* is the novel by Richard Blackmore, first published in 1869.

54   'some R.A.s' refers to members of the Royal Academy of Arts, the institution run by eminent artists and architects.

55   John Everett Millais, 1829-1896, was the English painter and illustrator, one of the founders of the Pre-Raphaelite Brotherhood.

56   'Ta-ra-ra Boom-de-ay' was the music hall song from 1880s USA and made popular in London in 1892 by Lottie Collins, who 'delivered the suggestive verses with deceptive demureness'.

57   Mary Anderson, 1859-1940, was the American stage actress who came to London to perform, and by 1892 had married Antonio Fernando de Navarro, settling in Worcestershire and becoming a hostess with a circle of musical, literary and ecclesiastical guests.

58   Lillie Langtry, 1853-1929, was an actress and producer. Her looks attracted interest, comment and invitations from artists and society hostesses.

59   Mrs Espinasse was the wife of the Rev. E. Espinasse, Vicar of Burmington.

60   W.H. Sinclair was producer/director of *Triple Bill*.

61   French's reference to 'waggeries' refers to his articles for *The Irish Cyclist* under the nom-de-plume 'Will Wagtale'.

62   French took lodgings here at The Mall, Strand Road, on the sea front, Baldoyle, from a Mrs Hanley. His rooms had views of the sea. The substantial house is still there in 2015. A short walk away was Sutton railway station.

63   Richard ('Dick') Orpen, 1863-1938, was a draughtsman, cartoonist, watercolour artist and architect, and the brother of William Orpen (1878-1931), the artist.

64   *The Irish Cyclist and Athlete* (I. C. & A.) was the magazine edited by R.J. Mecredy.

65   Marie Du Bédat, born in 1860, was the Dublin singer known in 1893 as 'The Irish Nightingale'. She toured England in Houston Collisson's *Concert Party*, turning to opera later, eventually moving to New York. She appears in Joyce's *Ulysses*, in the dream sequence as 'Miss Dubedatandshedidbedad'.

66   Priscilla Cecilia (1870-1941), later Countess Annesley, was the sister of French's first wife, Ethel. She married her first cousin Hugh Annesley, the fifth Earl, on 2 July 1892. They lived at Castlewellan House in Northern Ireland. She was considered one of the great beauties of her time and was photographed much by Alexander Bassano. She is not to be confused with the previous Countess Annesley (1808-1891), also confusingly named Priscilla Cecilia. The Annesley Hall in Newcastle was built in 1892 in memory of that earlier Countess.

67   'Stitched with care' is a parody of Thomas Moore's 'Rich and rare were the gems she wore' from his Irish melodies of 1808. A line by line comparison is instructive, so here is the original:

> Rich and rare were the gems she wore,
> And a bright gold ring on her wand she bore;
> But, O, her beauty was far beyond
> Her sparkling gems or snow-white wand.
>
> 'Lady! dost thou not fear to stray,
> So lone and lovely, through this bleak way?
> Are Erin's sons so good or so cold
> As not to be tempted by woman or gold?'
>
> 'Sir Knight! I feel not the least alarm,
> No son of Erin will offer me harm;
> For though they love woman and golden store,
> Sir Knight! they love honour and virtue more!'
>
> On she went, and her maiden smile
> In safety lighted her round the green isle;
> And blest forever is she who relied
> Upon Erin's honour and Erin's pride!

68   In the event Dr Collisson arranged a tour in the north, including Belfast, Downpatrick and Portadown. The programme consisted largely of operatic arias, popular ballads and violin solos. *The Belfast News Letter*, after the Ulster Hall concert on 6 December, wrote that 'Mr. Percy W. French's humorous songs and sketches were, if somewhat out of place at such a concert, none the less appreciated.' After the Downpatrick concert the following day the same newspaper wrote that 'The programme terminated with a humorous sketch by Mr. Percy French, entitled "Our Local Penny Readings". His personation of the ridiculous was most enjoyable.'

69   'M.M.' is *Midsummer Madness*.

70   Charles Mansergh was the opera singer and impresario who changed his name to Manners. His wife was Fanny Moody and their company was the *Moody-Manners Opera Company*. He had been an apprentice alongside French with the Midland Railway, and later created the role of Private Willis in *Iolanthe*. A distant cousin of his in 2015 is Martin Mansergh, the Irish public servant, historian and politician.

71   Loïe Fuller, 1862-1928, was a dancer in burlesque, vaudeville and circus shows. She combined her own choreography with silk costumes lit by multi-coloured lighting. Her Serpentine Dance, created in 1891, made her famous.

72   *The Second Mrs Tanqueray* is by Sir Arthur Wing Pinero.

73 Angelo Mascheroni, 1855-1905, was an Italian pianist, composer, conductor and teacher. He moved to London where several of his songs were published.

74 *Mat Hannigan's Aunt* has words and music by Percy French.

75 Richard Orpen's younger brother was William Orpen, to become the renowned Irish artist.

76 W.B. Yeats was living in London at this time, and had yet to write most of his poetry.

77 John Pigott was the Dublin publisher (J. Pigott & Sons) of 'Phil the Fluther's Ball', 'Slattery's Mounted Fut' and 'The Mountains of Mourne' amongst others.

78 William Lecky was the Dublin historian, pictured here with the monkey and evolutionary book. The slide was probably to introduce French's patter with lightning sketches 'How man was descended from the ape.'

79 The 1886 First Irish Home Rule Bill was defeated in the House of Commons; the 1893 Second Home Rule Bill was passed by the House of Commons, but vetoed in the House of Lords.

80 In this sketch of an amateur play the prompter takes the principal part, but this was lost on the *Dublin Independent* reviewer, writing that 'The prompter had more to do than perhaps ought to have fallen to his share, and even at times his unconspicuous office was kindly undertaken for him by the players themselves, who in this regard showed a praiseworthy reciprocity.' However, the writer continues, 'It must be recorded that Mr French's sketch is full of clever things, some of the best being the song Mat Hannigan's Aunt, which the author renders in fetching fashion, accompanying himself the while on the banjo.'

In spite of French's previous doubts about *Little Lord Faultyboy*, Collisson gets good praise from the same reviewer: 'The ease and self-confidence with which Dr W.H. Collisson donned the velvet tunic and lace of Little Lord Faultyboy proves that the "popular concert" organizer has developed a new talent, and his acting throughout was uncommonly good and at times most entertaining.'

81 Westland Row station, now named 'Dublin Pearse', was extensively rebuilt in 1891. Just to the east of Trinity College, and running through the college itself, the girders are part of the landscape.

82 *Charley's Aunt* is the farce by Brandon Thomas. This first London season ran to a record 1466 performances.

83 Geliebt in German means dearest, so Geliebtest is French's way of expressing 'Dearest dearest'.

84 A typescript of all three acts of *The Banshee* is in the memorabilia of the Percy French Society in Bangor Castle. It awaits a performance.

85 The Antient Concert Rooms, now The Academy Cinema, Pearse Street (formerly Brunswick Street), Dublin, was opened in 1844. It had a seating capacity of 600.

86 The Field Fisher Quartet comprised Evelyn Field-Fisher, Marjorie Field-Fisher, Alfred Field-Fisher and Eric Field-Fisher.

87 The painted doors of The Mall are no longer there: the one illustrated is in the Bangor archives and the other two were cut up, framed and sold by the Oriel Gallery.

88 In this staff photograph of *The Irish Cyclist* at top left is H.J. Holmes, who wrote under the nom-de-plume 'Philander'. His parodies and poems are well worth checking out.

89 The Dudley Gallery in 1892 was housed in the Egyptian Hall, Piccadilly, and gave its name to the *Dudley Gallery Art Society*.

90 Thomas German Reed, 1817-1888, founded the *German Reed Entertainment*, consisting of musical plays 'of a refined nature'.

91 A P.O.O. is a Post Office Order, later simply called a Postal Order, a way of sending money through the post.

92 French's poem 'Red-letter Days' includes the verse:

> Sweet Glenfinlas! I'm your debtor,
> For many a red letter
> Must mark the days we cycled by Lough Katrine's silver strand.
> Darrynane! thy sunset glory
> I have painted con amore,
> When she and I were members of Mecredy's merry band.

93 Cloonyquin was the family home where French was born. The house no longer exists, but there is a monument to French near the site.

94 French Park House, Co. Roscommon, was a Georgian house, since demolished.

95 'However I daresay she means well' is perhaps a reference to Lennie's mother, or more accurately stepmother, trying to come to terms with the fact that her young daughter is engaged to a man who only lost his wife two years previously? Or is it the age difference?

96 'shlaven si wole' is in German more correctly 'Schlafen sie wohl', meaning 'sleep well'.

97   *Music and Morals* was by the Rev. H.R. Haweis, 1839-1901. The book was first published in 1871 and ran to many editions.

98   'I am about £12 to the good' might not seem much to us today, but the average annual salary in 1892 was £60, so £12 is equivalent to over two months' salary.

99   *Tête montée* (French) means over-excited, agitated, worked up.

100   The Godleys' Irish home was The Rectory, Drominchin, Carrigallen, Co. Leitrim. Alfred's father, the Rev. James Godley, indirectly inspired the creation of 'Phil the Fluther's Ball', with his story of meeting the local flute player and hearing how he paid his rent.

101   Godley is an Oxford don, as opposed to a Spanish honorific Don, and French uses the Spanish female equivalent to refer to his wife.

102   12 Dawson Street was in the centre of Dublin. The building is no longer there, much of Georgian Dublin having been demolished in the 1960s and 1970s.

103   Joseph Joachim, 1831-1907, was the Hungarian violinist and composer who was one of the great violinists of the century. Schumann and Brahms wrote concertos for him.

104   'Gretchen Gretchen' is French's own version of the song 'Daisy, Daisy'. Daisy is a nickname for Margaret, and Gretchen a German pet form of Margaret.

105   Alyce Lindé's cutting includes these lines pertaining to the previous letter: 'Mr. W. Percy French was at his best in a delightfully funny sketch describing his attempts to get away from the popular song "Daisy Bell," the translation of the song into various European tongues was greeted with shrieks of delight.'

106   Crystal Palace was built on Sydenham Hill in 1854 and finally burnt down in 1931. The main hall held 4000.

107   *Chronicles* refers to the sketching class and 'his great power of imparting knowledge to others. Those who attended his sketching classes when he lived in Dublin felt this very much and used to thoroughly enjoy their expeditions with him to our many beauty spots. In fact he had only to walk along the stretch of canal on which his house was then situated to obtain lovely effects of sky, water and foliage. It was of that stretch that Ruskin said "To walk along it is a liberal education for an artist".'

108   Miss Whittle was Lennie's niece Mary, aged three, and Geoffrey Whittle Lennie's nephew, aged two, children of Lennie's sister Ethel.

109 French's first major London appearance had been in April, and was heralded in *The Era*: 'Mr W. Percy French, a new entertainer of a light and bright nature from the Emerald Isle, will make his first appearance in London, under very distinguished patronage, at the Steinway Hall on April 26th. Mr French's speciality is that, though his entertainments will be given *à la* Grossmith, they will consist wholly and solely of Irish characters and characteristics.'

110 Dr Paul Tribe, 1871-1954, nephew of Lennie's mother.

111 Relevant gravestones in the Church of St Barnabas and St Nicholas, Burmington, are as follows:

> In loving memory of Mary Clementina wife of Jonathan Sheldon who died December 24th 1869 aged 22 years.
>
> Also their infant son who was born and died May 29th 1867.
>
> Also of Jonathan Sheldon who died March 9th 1919 aged 77 years.
>
> And of Rosabel his 2nd wife who died January 10th 1908 aged 64 years.
>
> Jonathan's parents:
>
> In memory of Thomas Izod Sheldon who died April 11th 1878 aged 74 years.
>
> Also of Elizabeth wife of Thomas Izod Sheldon who died February 21st 1884 aged 77 years.
>
> Arthur son of Thomas and Elizabeth Sheldon who died March 25th 1847 aged 10 months.
>
> Also Henry son of the above who died May 26th 1847 aged 4 years.
>
> Catherine daughter of the above who died July 1st 1853 aged 15 years.

112 Percy French died of cardiac failure after seven days of bronchopneumonia, at Green Lea, College Avenue, Formby. His grave is at the Parish Church of Saint Luke, Church Road, Formby, just south of the church.

Select Bibliography

Collisson, W.A. Houston, *Dr. Collisson In and On Ireland* (London 1908)

Daly, Mrs de Burgh, ed., *Percy French, Chronicles and Poems*
    (Dublin, Talbot Press, 1922)

Daly, Mrs de Burgh, ed., *Prose, Poems and Parodies of Percy French*
    (Dublin, Talbot Press, 1925)

French, Ettie, *Willie* (Holywood, Percy French Society, 1994)

French, Percy, *Songs of Percy French, Volume 1* (London, Keith Prowse, 1957)

French, Percy, *Songs of Percy French, Volume 2* (London, Keith Prowse, 1957)

French, Percy, *The Irish Troubadour, More Songs of Percy French*
    (London, Keith Prowse, 1963)

Healy, James N., *Percy French and His Songs* (Cork, The Mercier Press, 1966)

Nulty, Oliver, *Lead Kindly Light* (Dublin, The Oriel Gallery, 2002)

O'Dowda, Brendan, *The World of Percy French* (Belfast, Blackstaff Press, 1981)

Tongue, Alan, *A Picture of Percy French* (Antrim, Greystone Press, 1990)

Index of Names

List of Watercolours

Oh, Mary, this London's a wonderful sight,
Wid the people here workin' by day and by night:
They don't sow potatoes, nor barley, nor wheat,
But there's gangs o' them diggin' for gold in the street —
At least, when I axed them, that's what I was told,
So I just took a hand at this diggin' for gold,
But for all that I found there, I might as well be
Where the Mountains o' Mourne sweep down to the sea.

My dearest Lennie

Your first love letter arrived this morning – it was short but sweet I am glad to hear you miss me, let me have more of your society when I re...

I he...

grea...

at...

terde...

blac...

fille...

I al...

to...

comp...

my...

Dearest Lennie

You can't [glad] I am off to Sheps... 10 train tomo... couldn't sta... after getting... letter. I only hope I won't be incarcerated as an escaped lunatic n route — I feel like me – but it is th delirium of joy. You

Beloved Lennie

Just a line now to tell you to keep up your spirits for you must be having a very trying time. & I will write again on Friday when the "Grand Concert" will be over. Just now I am trying to finish a couple of pictures (orders) practice choruses sketch from nature & work up some songs & recitations of my own so my mind is a little chaotic. I hope Aunt Bell is improving in health & spirits, & will soon be herself again.

The noble peasantry here think I have "improved wonderful" but "oh Marster Willie didn't ye get terrible grey". I think a ramble with you about this old place would be equal to the Downs which is saying a good deal

Chelsea S.W.

Dear Miss Sheldon

Do please write to me I was hoping for a line this morning but nothing came except letters from ...nts (theatrical) who ... anxious to make ... fortune.

... am only anxious ... thing — can you ever ... me ha...

The good ship Muenster ... Sunday. 8 bells. ...d astern. ...t'gan selo & royals ... t (except the writer ... is untaught)

... from the above ... high seas. And ...ne, fame & fortune. ...en lecturing on ...s, ...d W.S.F. as a com... ...cape world. I haven't ... ... the landlord of ... 12 'Sawsen Street yet, as he wants me to take another room as well as the studio, but I have a scheme on hand which may suit all parties. Ospen is going to set up an office for himself so I have just written to him to go & look at the other room, if he took it, it would be very pleasant to have such a congenial neighbour.

I have 7 pupils promised already ... ...my own sou... was over, it's very ... to think that I can make y... Well to tell you all that ...happened since I rode away ... gallant like. I didn't get to ... till 2.15. so found Collison ... to the Haymarket leaving he...